Feed A Family Of Four For As Low As $10.00 Per Week

And Enjoy A Nibble Of Independence

THROUGH SELF-SUFFICIENCY

By the Authors of

A Bite Of Independence

Marlynn Phipps
Jan Woolley
Venecia Phipps
&
Jenny Phipps

Dedicated to a wonderful mother and grandmother
Gladys Whiting
and to
all our other family members who have sacrificed and been so patient during the preparation of this book.

Photography by
Mark Hatch, Cathy Marshall & Jenny Phipps

Drawings by Gene Phipps

Printed in The United States Of America

Table Of Contents

9 Glorious Grains:

Wheat: Bread, Crackers and Pasta .... Page 28
Wheat Meat: The Money-saving Alternative .... Page 48
Corn: .... Page 60
Soybeans: A Dairy In a Bean .... Page 64
Rice: .... Page 71
Oats: .... Page 74
Rye: .... Page 77
Barley: .... Page 79
Millet: .... Page 80
Dried Beans: .... Page 81

In addition to recipes, you'll find directions for sprouting your own bean sprouts.

• **Bind It Together or Dress It Up** .... Page 85

This chapter features sauces, dressings, and condiments to make your foods sing to you, inexpensively. The addition of a chosen sauce can raise a dish from mediocre to magnificent. Throw away those expensive cans and learn to create your own for mere pennies.

• **Sumptuous Snacks, Soups and Sandwiches** .... Page 89

Quick and easy, these recipes will add a new dimension to lunchtime or snack time.

• **Satisfying The Sweet Tooth** .... Page 94

"Austerity" is a word we don't recognize on our program! We don't overlook the need for affordable, delicious goodies. Anyone can use a "warm fuzzy" occasionally, and this chapter's got 'em!

• **Produce Your Own Produce** .... Page 97

Fruits and vegetables are important to a well-balanced diet. This chapter will show you that, even in a restricted area, a garden is possible. With an emphasis on container gardening, you can grow your own nearly anywhere.

• **Putting Aside** .... Page 102

Here you find how easy it is to store your dried grains and beans. With the emphasis on dehydrating and freezing, you will learn how to keep for future use your produce and meats.

• **Fish Farming** ....Page 114

Who says you need a license to go fishing? Now you can fish in your own yard, anytime the mood strikes you. One of the most popular subjects at our seminars, fish farming will teach you how you can raise up to 200 pounds, yearly, of delicious, low-fat, inexpensive protein, even on a city lot!

• **Home Butchering** ....Page 116

Raising your own meat generally brings to mind the image of a beef steer. Rabbits, however, can be raised nearly anywhere and provide excellent, low cholesterol meat. For those too squeamish to butcher their own, information is given on how being your own home butcher can save you money on supermarket purchases.

• **Cheese And Yogurt** ....Page 119

Our grandparents had the best, freshest dairy products and now we can, too. Using modern technology, the yummiest yogurts and creamiest cheeses can be easily made at the fraction of the cost of store-bought. Step-by-step guides and suggestions for using are found in this chapter.

• **Veggie Treats** ....Page 127

(Guaranteed Pleasers For Those Who Didn't Think They Liked Them) Vegetables lend their nutrition joyfully to a meal with these proven favorite side dishes.

• **Beekeeping -** Nature's Sweet Bounty at a Honey of a Price .Page 130

With a minimum of investment in equipment or time, you can put thousands of energetic workers to work for you... providing you and your family with all the sweetening you desire.

• **The Leftover Question** ....Page 138

What to do with those little tidbits growing green fuzz in the back of the refrigerator? This section addresses the age old question and provides novel, economical answers. Nothing ever needs to be wasted, and you will be amazed at the results. Fruit peelings and cores become vinegars, and pan scrapings and meat scraps become soup stocks, soup bases and gelatins. All these and many more can be obtained from what is normally thrown away.

• **Make Up Your Own Make-up and More** .... Page 144

A good portion of the budget goes toward non-food items such as soaps and cosmetics. Here you will find easy recipes for making such things as fine hand soaps and shampoos, plus cosmetics and toothpaste.

• **Miscellaneous** .... Page 147

This chapter has a lot in common with the old "General Store", for it has a little bit of everything, from laundry soap and cleaning supplies, to spice mixes and seasoning charts (See pages 154 - 157).

• **What If. . . ?** .... Page 154

This chapter, although difficult to think about, can lend a great peace of mind. It doesn't take a natural disaster such as an earthquake or flood to wish for preparedness. What if your source of income were suddenly cut off? We have learned from past disasters that there is generally a 72 hour interval before the government gets everything in gear to help affected individuals. In this chapter you will learn tips on what to store, how to plan, even first-aid, if needed. The feeling of security that comes from being prepared knows no price.

• **Index** .... Page 157

Introduction

Feed a Family of Four For As Low As $10.00 Per Week **And Enjoy A <u>Nibble</u> of Independence? . . .** The first thing that comes to many minds is, What an odd title!" An explanation is in order as to how this all came about.

Our initial project was a large, comprehensive book which, after considerable thought, we titled ***Feed a Family of Four For As Low As $10.00 Per Week And Enjoy A <u>Bite</u> of Independence***. This was in response to people who, when attending our seminars, would exclaim, "Oh, you are writing a cookbook!" We would hasten to explain that we are writing a **Way Of Life** book that happened to contain numerous favorite recipes.

Much More Than A Cookbook

The concept far exceeded the scope of a mere cookbook. You see, we teach that self-sufficiency is possible for anyone, even on a suburban lot. This entails not only cooking techniques and recipes, but the growing of your own vegetables and learning to process and store what you grow. We teach you how to raise fish in a nearly free ecosystem in your own back yard and how to save money butchering your own meat. (Rabbits, for example, can be raised in the city - even indoors - and they provide excellent, low cost protein.) Keeping bees is a project with a minimal investment in time, yet even a city dweller can provide the family's annual sweetening needs.

We are proud to say we can teach how to feed a family of four for as low as $10.00 a week. In keeping with the claim, we teach money-saving procedures in addition to recipes. Into this whole concept goes the making of your own soaps and cosmetics from materials usually thrown away. Making your own delicious cheeses, generally too expensive to purchase, is described in detail. And a low cost, yet nutritious, alternative to meat is found in the liberal use of "Wheat Meat" which, when used in our recipes, is nearly impossible to tell from the real thing.

Other grains, not frequently used by most, find their delicious entry into our menus, allowing money left for the inclusion of meat for those who enjoy it.

What we teach is not an austerity program, but a joyful, satisfying living concept. A section on sweets is even included for those who have the insatiable sweet tooth. The fact that a number of them, being based on soy, are actually healthful, is an added bonus.

To make it all practical and less intimidating, we provide steps on what to store and how to use it. Sample menus make planning simple, and a section on leftovers even helps you to use economically whatever might remain. Tying it together is a section on time management showing how anyone can accomplish this lifestyle with forethought and ease.

So therefore ***Feed A Family Of Four For As Low As $10.00 Per Week And Enjoy A Bite Of Independence Through Self-Sufficiency*** seemed to us the perfect title for a book that provided not only a healthful way of eating, but independence from the long lines at the store, hours in traffic, and the ever-tightening noose of rising supermarket prices.

This book, a broad sampling of what is found in the larger ***Bite Of Independence,*** is thus subtitled ***A Nibble Of Independence***, and we hope that you enjoy its flavor!

For more information on any item in this book, please write:

P. O. Box 2050
Higley, AZ 85236-2050

Feeding A Family Of Four For As Low As $10 A Week

It's not impossible
And it's not beyond your abilities

Here's how the concept evolved. . . and how it can work for you!

The seeds of this book were sown nearly 12 years ago when Marlynn Phipps and her family were living on a farm in Missouri's Ozark Mountains.

At that time, Missouri in general and the Ozarks in particular had become a kind of Mecca for hundreds of people in search of a back-to-the-land way of life. In their enthusiasm, and sometimes desperation, these people had sold all their possessions and found themselves ill-prepared for the rural living style of their forebears. The result was widespread hardship, with families struggling simply to feed themselves.

By contrast, Marlynn's background had prepared her well to live off the land. Her father had died before her birth, and she and her 5 brothers and sisters were raised by an indomitable mother whose resourcefulness seemed to know no limitations. Armed with skills handed down from her mother-in-law, this woman taught her family all she knew. The ability to make something out of nearly nothing was the legacy she left them, and when hard times came, they managed to manage well.

This approach to life frequently led Marlynn to experiment in the kitchen. She was intrigued by grains and their multitude of possible uses. Wheat was of particular interest, since its insoluble protein, gluten, could be formed and flavored in countless ways. She worked and refined the technique and thus "wheat meat" was born.

Marlynn's abilities did not go unnoticed. Approached by a prominent area clergyman, she was asked to demonstrate her skills to other families as a way of alleviating their suffering. This she did with enthusiasm and many people were helped through some difficult times.

The $10-A-Week Concept Takes Shape

Throughout those early years, an idea was taking shape in Marlynn's mind: the notion that people could be fed nutritiously and economically by using one pound of grain per person, per day, and that, by supplementing the diet with produce from even a small garden, a well-balanced diet was possible for mere pennies.

Strict vegetarianism was not the goal, however. By following this plan, Marlynn envisioned that enough money could be saved to make meat affordable, in moderation, and moderation as we've learned recently is one of the keys to good health.

This concept, as it took form, encompassed more than a heavy reliance on grains. It entailed living a whole way of life in which each part contributed to the whole. Skills which had been handed down for generations and largely abandoned by most people today, were dusted off. Surprisingly, a number of them find application in today's fast-paced, fast-food world.

The resulting recipes in this book reflect the years of trial and error, and it is with some pride we claim that people attending our seminars today are hard pressed to tell wheat meat from the real thing; which perfume is an expensive brand and which is concocted in the kitchen from fresh flowers; which laundry soap costs a small fortune and which one is made from fat scraps normally discarded.

The Heritage Is Handed Down

Today finds Marlynn comfortable in the present due to her knowledge of the past and her heritage is being handed down to her daughters, Jenny and Venecia.

A competent cook since she was 7 years old and first began demonstrating in her mother's seminars, Jenny, now at 16, has poise and confidence in front of both TV cameras and large audiences. When not on the road she can be found, as her mother before her, experimenting in the kitchen. We call her our "kitchen chemist", for from her efforts has come an array of custom-blended fragrances and subtle, to dramatic cosmetics - not to mention original foods of all description.

When presented with a challenge, Jenny's response is "If it isn't as good or better than the commercial product, don't bother!" So far she has yet to let anyone down.

Venecia's talents do not take a back seat to her sister's, although she generally seeks a less visible role. Profoundly deaf from birth, she doesn't know the meaning of the word "handicap". Her skilled lip reading and quick grasp of a situation, coupled with a surprisingly well modulated voice, amaze people meeting her for the first time.

Seminars would not proceed nearly so smoothly without Venecia's behind-the-scene assistance. She, too, is a competent and innovative cook, contributing many of the recipes found in this book.

Her love for animals explains the relaxation she finds in caring for the family's flock of chickens, and she is well repaid by the fresh eggs they all enjoy.

Teaming Up

People of similar interests seem to find each other, and so it seemed inevitable that Jan Woolley and Marlynn and her daughters should eventually meet and become friends.

Jan, with an academic background in zoology and animal husbandry from Brigham Young University and Arizona State University, is a single mother raising four young sons.

In the interest of providing a good environment and back-to-basics life for her children, she is practicing the same skills Marlynn has grown up with.

For example . . .

A flock of chickens provides both meat and eggs for her table as well as a small supplemental income.

Her sheep give not only their wool for spinning projects, but also lambs which she butchers and with which she fills her freezer. From their home-tanned skins she fashions fleecy caps and vests.

Owning a family cow more than provides for her family's needs. Surplus milk is transformed into cream cheese, yogurt, butter, and dozens of kinds of cheeses - the sales of which offset the cost of feed.

To produce milk, a cow needs to be bred, so every year a home-butchered beef joins the lamb and chicken in Jan's freezer.

By-products are never wasted, for fat becomes fine scented soaps and hand-dipped tallow candles, while intestines are turned into natural casings for delicious homemade sausages.

One by-product people try to ignore is manure. Rather than consider it a disposal problem, Jan views it as a valuable commodity and uses it to return nutrients to her vegetable and flower gardens and fruit trees. The surplus is shredded, bagged, and sold by one of her sons.

This self-sufficient ecosystem is practiced on a one acre lot. We realize that not everyone has the same facilities, but with a blending of their ideas and combined experiences, Marlynn, Jenny, Venecia, and Jan will show you how it is possible to live happily and inexpensively, even in a city setting.

It's Worth Trying

Initially, the ideas presented in this book may seem a bit overwhelming. Remember, though, that with practice comes proficiency. In a very short time you will find these techniques becoming second nature and that this way of living is actually much easier than going to the store where traffic, long lines, and high costs must be faced. The savings realized can amount to hundreds of dollars every month. These dollars can be applied to the purchase of equipment which, in turn, make the tasks even quicker, easier and more simple.

So you see, by having a food storage program, growing a few fresh vegetables, focusing your time, and utilizing the techniques and tips in this book, you really can **FEED A FAMILY OF FOUR FOR AS LOW AS $10 A WEEK**, cheaper and easier than going to the store.

The First Step: Preparation

Your first step in preparation was the purchase of this book. What might at first seem to be an overwhelming task, becomes a lot less intimidating when broken down into manageable units.

Crucial to the success of this program is the use of planned food storage. Although we suggest a year's supply be set away, we realize not everyone is able to achieve that goal. Start with a three month's, or six month's supply and gradually build it up with the savings you will realize.

Grains: The Foundation

When thinking of food storage, one's thoughts turn to grains for they are inexpensive and easily stored. (It has been said that grain found in some of the Egyptian tombs actually germinated, thousands of years later.) In addition to being highly nutritious, grains have the ability to assume many forms, providing a varied and delicious diet. While this book's intent is not to promote vegetarianism, many vegetarians do find this approach to be ideal.

Our plan suggests that one pound a day of grain (in different forms or combinations) supplemented with home grown garden vegetables (See Produce section), can provide complete nourishment for one adult for one day.

In the United States the most popular grains are: Wheat, Corn, Rye, Oats, Rice, Barley, and Millet.

For the sake of convenience, we will also include Soybeans and other Dry Beans in our discussion of grains.

Taking advantage of grains' storability is one area of economic advantage. Buy them in bulk for greater savings and break them down into manageable quantities at home for your storage and use. Buing, directly from farmer through Farmer's Co-operatives (check with your County Extension Agent), or grain houses, are two sources for bulk grains. Another possible source would be Grains Plus. Write P. O. Box 2050, Higley, AZ 85236-2050 for current price list. In the "Putting Aside" chapter we will show you how simple a task it is.

Grains, by themselves, however, cannot make up a complete storage program. For the sake of palatability and good nutrition, several other items should be included.

We suggest that for one adult for one year the following list is a good guideline:

Suggested Amounts To Store

- 365 pounds of assorted grains, based on your family's eating habits
- 10 pounds of iodized salt
- 30 pounds of non-iodized salt if you do pickling or meat curing
- 25 pounds of fats or oils
- 50 pounds of sugar or honey
- 25 pounds Milk♥Lite®† or soybeans
- 5 pounds total of various soup bases, such as beef, chicken or fish. . there are many to choose from
- Various flavorings such as chocolate or carob, strawberry, etc.
- Herbs and spices of your choice, such as dehydrated onions, garlic, oregano, sage, cinnamon, etc.*

Once again, the amounts will depend upon your family's preferences.

† We recommend, for economy's sake, purchasing Milk♥Lite® in 50# bags. For information write P. O. Box 2050, Higley, AZ 85236-2050

* Bulk spices may be obtained from Sahuaro Spices Co. Write to: 3611 N. 34th Ave. Phoenix, AZ 85017, for price list.

Where Do I Put It All?

One might be tempted to shudder at the thought of finding room to store all these foodstuffs. With a little imagination it is possible to find, or create the room. Attractive items such as homemade soaps and decorative jars of dehydrated fruits and vegetables can accent the wall when displayed on an open shelf. For that matter, shelves, themselves, can be constructed of 5 gallon buckets or storage cans and 1 inch lumber. Cover the buckets with contact paper, or stain and paint to match your decor. Accent tables can be made by grouping or stacking several cans together and topping them with a circular piece of plywood, covering all with a large piece of coordinating fabric to reach the floor. Under the bed is an often over-looked storage area, and it is a perfect environment for items that require dry, dark storage.

Can I Do It In MY Kitchen?

With food obtained, and securely stored, preparation is nearly complete. The last thing remaining is preparation itself, and here we turn to the kitchen.

While most procedures can be done by hand, you will find that to live this lifestyle in the manner most of us are accustomed to today, up-to-date electric appliances are essential. (In fact, that is one of the charms of this program: The results are hardly discernible from the things you love and are already used to!) The savings afforded by living this way will allow you to purchase equipment that truly makes it easier than going to the store.

Since so much depends upon the use of grains, a good mill is required. They come in all sizes and prices. Some are even convertible to hand power in the event of a power failure. Some are in attractive wood cabinets where they accent the kitchen, and some are small and easily tucked away in a cupboard. The flour, when produced on-the-spot from your own home stored grain, is far superior in flavor and nutrition to that purchased pre-ground and stale from the store.

Next to be considered is a heavy duty electric mixer. Most of the better models nowadays have wonderful attachments, the meat or food grinder being one we most frequently use. Even available are pasta-making attachments which make easy the fun pastas we all love so. (Did you ever try whole wheat, freshly ground, pasta? It has no equal!)

An electric blender deserves a place on your counter, for its uses are many and varied.

Rounding out the requirements for a fully prepared kitchen are the colanders, bowls, and normal utensils used in food preparation.

Now, you have your foodstuffs, you have it stored well, and your kitchen is all set to go. The question remains, "How the heck do I do it all! Do I really have the time?" Fortunately, the answer is **YES!**

Make The Clock Work For You

Next to "yum!", one of the most frequent comments we hear from people who attend our seminars is, "How on Earth do you find the time!". We couldn't dare make the claim that living our program is ". . . easier and quicker than going to the store. . ." if we didn't find it to be true.

Many of our shortcuts and hints have evolved naturally through trial and error. A few would appear to some as being nothing more than common sense, yet frequently that same person might say, "Why didn't I think of that myself?". If time management were to be summed up in two words, they would be **PREPLANNING** and **SIMPLIFICATION**.

Before retiring for the night it is helpful to make a mental note, if not an actual list, of the morrow's activities. For example, you might put soybeans out to soak for tomorrow's tofu-making or perhaps set out a sourdough starter to begin working. By preplanning you won't be facing the next day saying, "If only I had done. . ."

There will always be the unanticipated interruptions - possibly even emergencies - but if you set your course the night before, the next day's sailing goes a lot smoother. As a personal note, we find it provides a mental boost - it might even be said, a physical boost - to tackle some particularly distasteful job the first thing in the morning. The remainder of the day can therefore be so much more productive by just completing that one task you would have rather put off.

"Homework" Can Be Fun

There is a difficult distinction that needs to be clarified here in order to understand our program. Much of our preplanning involves labor at home in the production of what would have been required to drive to the store to purchase. So what you are doing is allowing yourself the luxury of remaining at home to create the staples for which you would have had to pay in time and dollars, gasoline, and wear and tear. Just say to yourself, "Time on the road = time at home, and the savings are bigger, to boot!"

This principle prompts our suggestion that one afternoon every two weeks be set aside for the making of such staples as cereals, sauces, spice mixes, convenience mixes, mayonnaise, mustards, etc. Other simplifying chores such as grating large quantities of cheese at one time, to be frozen in recipe-size portions, could be performed at this time.

We will use a couple of examples to illustrate this point, wheat meat and sauces: It would be tedious, indeed, to make wheat meat everyday. But one of the nice things about wheat meat is the fact that it can be frozen successfully at nearly any state of preparation. We depend heavily upon a freezer for maximizing the time spent in the kitchen. If a freezer is unavailable, the procedures remain basically the same; they just have to be done more often. So spend a morning making wheat meat (it is as easy to make up several batches as it is to make one), and in a matter of time you will have filled your freezer with "roasts", "ground beef", "chicken", "shrimp" and more. We all know how versatile these various cuts of "meat" can be when planning a variety of meals. We might liken wheat meat to the Basic Black Dress women used to be encouraged to buy: dress it up, or down, with various accessories and it was as if a whole wardrobe had been purchased for the cost of that one dress.

In the same genre are found the sauces. They are the accessories to that black dress, for with the right sauce, wheat meat can duplicate nearly anything. Many sauces employ the same techniques in their preparation. With repetition comes familiarity, and with familiarity - speed. It doesn't take much time then to concentrate on making sauces and before long, the freezer contains many "makings" for delightful dinners, at a fraction of the cost and time.

Time Saving Tips

This might be the time to mention a few tips that cut time in the kitchen. The first would be to **CLEAN UP AS YOU GO**. If you are using bowls or pans, place the largest dirty one in the sink, filled with hot soapy water. Then as you dirty them, nest other utensils, etc, in the soapy water and when your job is complete, the dishes are practically washed by themselves. It is a matter of a quick swish and a rinse and you are not staggered by an insurmountable pile of dirty, dried-on, crusty dishes. We might say the same about leaving the dishes in the sink or on the counter over-night. There are a lot more pleasant things to wake up to in the morning than an overwhelming mess. The whole day begins a lot more productively if a few more minutes are taken at night. Wipe-ups are considered in this same light. Keep a sponge on the sink and as spills are made on the counter, wipe them up immediately. While they are soft and fresh, it only takes a second yet saves considerable time and exasperation later. By cooking in this fashion, not only does the kitchen stay uncluttered, but the mind and attitude, also.

A second tip would be to **MINIMIZE BOWLS AND UTENSILS**. While it may sound contrary to what we have just discussed, if you can reuse a bowl without affecting the subsequent project, do it. For example, when making bread there is really no need to wash the bowl before starting pasta. As you cook you will find where many times this principle may be applied. In our cooking we make "one-bowl" recipes out of many that would have you filling a whole counter with utensils.

BREAKING A TASK INTO MANAGEABLE UNITS would be tip number three. We put up a whole crop's worth of peas in the freezer without much of a break in normal routine by simply picking a bowl full every morning as they ripened. It didn't take long to pick, blanch and freeze one bowl. (Not all vegetables are as accommodating, however. Tomatoes come on like gangbusters and this is when it is nice to know that tomatoes can be washed and frozen, whole, to be used or processed at a more convenient time.)

Lastly, we would mention that art of **INTERLOCKING VARIOUS TASKS.** We call it an art because it is something that is learned, although it is not terribly difficult to do.

A GREAT EQUATION: 2 1/2 HOURS LABOR = 1 WEEK LEISURE

Jenny showed us a good example of all these procedures the other day. Within two and one-half hours one morning, she single-handedly prepared twenty-one meals - a whole week's worth - and had them tucked away in the freezer and refrigerator before noon.

Can you imagine the ease and freedom this kind of management gives to the remainder of the week?

This is a good time to remind you that, as of this writing, Jenny is only 16 years old. We are fond of telling people "If a teenage girl can do it, so can you!". Granted, Jenny has had practice, but everyone has to begin somewhere. You may not be as proficient in the beginning, but look what can be done.

Here is what she prepared that morning, and following is a brief outline of her sequence. The procedures and recipes are found in the index:

1. **LASAGNA** *
2. **SPAGHETTI WITH WHEAT MEATBALLS** *
3. **CHILI MAC**
4. **ONE DOZEN CORN TORTILLAS FOR ENCHILADA DINNER**
5. **HOMINY CASSEROLE**
6. **TWO CHEESE PIZZAS**
7. **TURKEY & DRESSING**
8. **CHICKEN STRIPS**
9. **CHICKEN CHUNK CASSEROLE**

10. **CHICKEN SALAD**
11. **SHRIMP**
12. **GROUND BEEF PATTIES FOR SALISBURY-TYPE STEAKS**
13. **LEFT OVER GROUND BEEF FOR IMPROMPTU DINNER**
14. **WAFFLE MIX (GROUND WHEAT, OATS, BARLEY)**
15. **TOFU CREPES MIX**
16. **TOFU FOR 2 EXTENDED-EGG BREAKFASTS**
17. **THREE BREAKFASTS OF HOMEMADE CEREAL**
18. **THREE LOAVES WHOLE GRAIN BREAD**

* All the pasta dishes, plus 2 pizza crusts were based on a one gallon batch of spaghetti sauce.

A 16 Year Old Did What??

She began with the making of wheat meats, and since unbleached flour is used to simulate pork, shrimp, poultry and fish, this was the logical starting point. So, while a 14 Cup batch was kneading on the mixer's dough hook, she turned to the making of the dark wheat meat used in simulating ham, beef, and some poultry.

Pouring 8 Cups of wheat (the first installment of 16 Cups she was to grind), into the mill, she left it to grind while she set the corn and lime on the stove to cook for the masa (used for tortillas), and hominy.

At this point, the white flour was sufficiently mixed so it was removed from the mixer and placed in cool water to rest. (During this time the 2nd installment of wheat was poured into the mill to grind.)

The removal of the white dough freed the mixer which was then filled with freshly ground wheat (the 1st installment's worth, around 12 Cups flour), for the making of the dark wheat meat. (There was no need to take the time to wash the mixer bowl, as the doughs are similar.) The mixing of this dough began as with the earlier white batch.

By this time the white dough had rested sufficiently to begin the washing process, and the resulting starch water was poured into containers set aside to be used later for bread-making and thickening. The washed gluten (wheat meat) was set aside, covered with cool water, to await further treatment.

The dark wheat dough was now placed in the same colander just vacated by the white and allowed to rest in cool water while she used the 2nd installment of wheat flour and some of the starch water to make whole-grain bread. (Once again, there was no need to wash any utensils.)

While the bread dough was kneading on the mixer's dough hook, she washed the bran and starch from the dark wheat meat with the same procedure used for the white earlier. As before, the water was saved and the dark gluten (wheat meat), was set aside in cool water to await further treatment.

With the whole-grain bread dough now kneaded, she separated enough dough to form 2 pizza crusts and the remainder was formed into 3 loaves. The loaves, now covered with damp cloths, were set aside to rise while the pizza crusts were popped into the oven to partially pre-bake. (They will be thawed and treated as "brown and serve" to top and reheat later.)

By this time the corn on the stove was ready to check for doneness. Testing cooked, it was rinsed well and masa ground, tortillas pressed and hominy prepared.

At this point she drew a breath and started on the preparation of pasta. Using 5 Cups of unbleached flour, 6 eggs and the still-unwashed-utensils, she mixed her pasta dough. From this batch she formed her lasagne noodles, macaroni, and spaghetti.

Now, with everything under control either resting, rising, or baking, she turned to the making of soy milk and tofu. The previously soaked beans were put in the blender and the process was followed which turned them into soy milk.

While the soy milk was cooking, and later, the tofu pressing, Jenny made her sauces for the pastas and enchiladas. (She could have thawed previously prepared and frozen ones. . .)

The final steps consisted of forming the wheat meats into the various forms required for each meal.

The morning's efforts were truly a case of fine-tuned management and familiarity with procedures and recipes. But with practice comes familiarity, and it won't be long before you, too, can make the clock work for you.

Magnificent Menus For Minimal Money

This section is designed as an aid in helping you to plan your menus. Care has been taken to combine proteins where wheat meat is used to assure that complete proteins are formed. This can be accomplished by the addition of soy products, cheeses or other dairy products, beans, eggs, or nuts.

We rely heavily upon home-grown produce to balance our diets while staying within the budgetary guidelines. The "Produce Your Own Produce" section gives many tips to enable nearly anyone to at least supplement the diet with home-grown, and where this might not be possible, we refer to vegetables and fruits "in season". This implies whatever is plentiful and cheap at the time in your particular area, or whatever you have "put aside".

For those without access to fresh milk (for cheesemaking, etc.), beehives or chickens, allow for differences in suggested costs. Where the word "beverage" is used, we refer to one or more of the following: Milk, "**Milk♥Lite**®", Soy Milk (generally flavored with chocolate, vanilla, or some other flavoring for palatability), or "Free For Nothing 'Coffee'", found in the "Wheat" . . . section of this book.

Asterisks (*), are used to denote recipes found elsewhere in the book which can be located in the index.

This is simply a guide; there are a number of recipes to be found within the book, plus procedures to permit you to "strike out on your own." It won't be long before you are comfortably and confidently "Feeding a Family of Four For as Low as $10.00 a Week".

SUNDAY

BREAKFAST:	Fruit, in season	* Hot Toast
	* Tofu-extended scrambled eggs	* Beverage
LUNCH:	* Quesadilla	* Pinto beans
	Fruit in season	* Beverage
DINNER:	* Spaghetti & Wheat Meatballs	* Baguettes
	Green or sprouted salad/Tofu Dressing	
	* Buttery Yellow Cake (1/4 of cake)	* Beverage

MONDAY

BREAKFAST: Fruit in Season
* Hot buttered homemade toast
* Great Nutties / milk
* Beverage

LUNCH: * Corn Stuffed Tomatoes
* Homemade Crackers
* Beverage

DINNER: * Wheat Meat Chimichangas/ with lettuce, tomato, tofu sour cream and cheese garnish
* Refritos II
Fruit in Season
* Beverage

TUESDAY

BREAKFAST: * Hot Whole-grain cereal / milk or **Milk♥Lite**®
* Hot buttered homemade toast
Fruit in Season
* Beverage

LUNCH: * Wheat Meat Cheeseburger/lettuce or sprouts
* Catsup, * Mustard, * Mayonnaise
French Fries
* Beverage

DINNER: * Tofu Stuffed Green Pepper
Frozen or Fresh Corn
Sprouted or green salad/ * Tofu dressing
* Apricot Tofu Ice Cream
* Wheat Bread
* Beverage

WEDNESDAY

BREAKFAST: Fruit in season
* Oat n' Wheat Waffle
* 'Free for Nothing Coffee'

LUNCH: * Wheat Meat Hot Dogs/ * cheese
French Fries
* Mayonnaise, Mustard, Catsup
* Beverage

DINNER: * Wheat Meat Shrimp/ * Cocktail Sauce
* Cottage Cheese & Fruit
Vegetable in season
* Buttery Yellow Cake (1/4)
* Beverage

THURSDAY

BREAKFAST
Oatmeal
* Tofu Extended Scrambled Eggs
* On Hand Bran Muffins
Apple Sauce
* Beverage

LUNCH:
* French Onion soup
* Wheat Meat Lunchmeat Sandwich
* Beverage

DINNER:
* Wheat Meat Turkey with dressing
Vegetable in Season
* Beverage
* Brown Rice
Fruit in Season

FRIDAY

BREAKFAST:
* Tofu Crepes/Fruit filling
* Hot Buttered Toast
* Beverage

LUNCH:
* Sloppy Joes, Wheat Meat style/* Hamburger buns
Green or sprouted salad/* Tofu dressing
* Beverage

DINNER:
Grilled home-raised fish
* Southern Style Cornbread
* Buttery Yellow Cake (1/4)
Rice
Vegetable in Season
* Beverage

SATURDAY

BREAKFAST:
* Oat n' Wheat Waffle/ Fruit in Season
* Tofu Extended Scrambled Eggs
* Beverage

LUNCH:
* Baked Beans
* Beverage
* Toasted Whole Wheat Triangles with * Cheese

DINNER:
* "Free Meal" Soup
* Homemade Crackers
Green or sprouted salad/*Tofu dressing
* Custard Crumb Pudding (made with last 1/4 cake)
* Beverage

No Time For Breakfast? Think Again!

Breakfast is an oft over-looked meal nowdays. People seem to feel there is just not enough time with the busy schedules most of us maintain, to accommodate this most important of meals. Studies have shown that work productivity and attention span is greater when a good breakfast has been consumed, so it greatly benefits adults as well as children to enjoy a good breakfast. "Ah, well and great," you say, "but I really do not have the time." . . . Relax and enjoy some of these time saving recipes and tips for a wholesome breakfast.

In days past, a hearty breakfast consisted of bowls of hot, steaming cereal, plus platters of eggs, rashers of bacon or sausage and hot breads of some type. While delicious, our styles of eating have changed over the years due in great part to the amount of time involved - (not to mention dietary concerns.)

The following are three methods of assuring yourself that traditional bowl of steaming hot cereal in the morning. Surely one of them will fit into your schedule.

Steamed Whole Grain (cereal)

2 Cups clean whole grain **3 Cups water**
1½ teaspoons salt

Put the whole grain in a heatproof bowl. Add water and salt. Place bowl, uncovered, on a rack in a large kettle containing 2 to 3 inches of water. Bring the water in the kettle to a boil, cover the kettle with the lid and after 15 minutes turn to low heat. Let steam 4 to 5 hours, or overnight.

Double Boiler Method

Put 1 Cup cracked grain in the top part of a double boiler with 3 or 4 Cups of water (if you desire) and 1 teaspoon of salt. Cook for 1 hour over medium heat.

OR. . .

Put the above ingredients in the top of a double boiler the evening before. Cook 30 minutes, remove from heat and resume cooking for 30 additional minutes the following morning.

Thermos Method

The morning before, put 1 Cup whole or cracked grain in a saucepan with enough water to cover about 1 inch deep. That evening add enough water to equal 3 Cups. Add 1 teaspoon salt and bring to a boil. Pour into a preheated Thermos, cap tightly and place it on its side. Enjoy the next morning.

NOTE: For variety, replace the cooking water with fresh milk, soy milk, Milk♥Lite®, or cook with raisins or other dried fruit.

Cold cereals - Always a Favorite

We know that we are not alone in our observation that most children would prefer a breakfast of nothing but cold cereal. With all the media hype and the convenience it affords the parent, no wonder. But the expense can be staggering, to say nothing of the nutrition that is lost in today's "sugar smackies". The following are some cold cereals that are not only healthful, but fun to let your children make themselves. The difficulty lies in keeping them from being eaten as fast as they are made.

Whole Wheat Flakes

2 Cups whole wheat flour
2 Cups water
1 teaspoon salt
1/2 Cup brown sugar

Mix ingredients with a spoon until the consistency of thin paint. Pour onto a greased baking sheet. Tip the sheet to cover the surface with a film, pouring the excess back into the bowl. Bake 350° about 15 minutes until crisp and golden. Pull off sheet and let cool before breaking into flakes. If desired, add bits of dried fruit and store in an airtight jar.

Oat Flakes

2 Cups oat flour*
1/4 Cup whole wheat flour
1½ Cups water
1 teaspoon salt
1/4 Cup brown sugar
1/4 Cup soy flour (See index)

* (Put rolled or groat oats through mill on fine grind)

Follow the procedure for the wheat flakes, but due to the fine texture of the oat flour, you may have to adjust the amount of water. An almost syrup-like consistency is desired. Pour thinly on the sheet, for if too thick, it becomes leathery instead of crisp. For variety add 1/2 teaspoon of cinnamon to the batter.

Merrios

1/4 Cup wheat starch*
1/4 Cup brown sugar
1 teaspoon baking soda
1/2 teaspoon salt
2 Cups or more of oat flour
1/4 Cup barley flour †
2 teaspoons malt powder
1 Tablespoon baking powder

* See Wheat Meat section for directions

† Run pearled, or whole barley through the mill on fine grind

Mix dry ingredients together. Work in the wheat starch which has been cooked over low heat to a thick paste. The dough should be stiff. Put through pasta machine on macaroni setting, let extrude in long strips. Lay on baking sheet and chop into desired lengths. If lacking a pasta machine, roll very thinly and place on sheet. Bake at 325° until crisp. When cool break into pieces and store in tightly covered container.

Bran Flakes

See the Wheat Meat section on Gluten Water for discussion of bran. To obtain the bran water needed for this recipe, pour off all but 1 inch of water covering the bran sediment in the container. If you lack the 6 Cups required for this recipe, it may be frozen until enough is accumulated to be baked at a later date.

6 Cups bran water
1/3 Cup honey or brown sugar
1 3/4 teaspoons salt

Mix the ingredients well and pour 1/2 Cup onto a greased baking sheet. Tip the sheet to spread the liquid evenly in the pan. Bake 30 minutes in a 350° oven until crisp. Watch carefully that it doesn't burn. Break into flakes and store in an airtight jar. These are delicious mixed with cinnamon or nutmeg.

Great Nutties

3 Cups sifted whole wheat flour
1/2 Cup barley flour †
1 teaspoon soda
3/4 Cup brown sugar
3/4 teaspoon salt
2 Cups milk*

* Sour the milk with 2 Tablespoons of lemon juice or vinegar

† Run pearled, or whole barley through the mill on fine grind

Mix dry ingredients together. Stir in the milk until well blended. Spread dough 1/4 inch thick on a greased cookie sheet. Bake 15 minutes at 375°. Let cool, then run through the meat grinder or food chopper. Return to the oven to complete drying, stirring to assure it doesn't burn. It needs to just toast lightly. Let cool thoroughly, then store in an airtight jar.

One might find an occasional person who doesn't like cold cereal. For that person, wherever he might be, here are some alternative ideas.

Alternative Breakfasts

1. Save leftover pancakes in freezer until you have a sufficient amount. In the morning, roll a pancake around a cooked sausage link and heat in the skillet or microwave. Serve with applesauce and cinnamon or maple syrup.

2. Spread a homemade flour tortilla, **(See index)** with hot scrambled eggs. Lay a slice of canned green chile and a strip of homemade cheese alongside and roll up. Top with salsa, **(See index).**

3. Bake apples the day before, stuffed with raisins, brown sugar and cinnamon. In the morning, nest the apple in a bowl of hot cooked cereal, prepared the night before. Serve with milk, soy milk or Milk♥Lite®.

Drink it on the Run

For the ultimate in a hurry-up breakfast, there are the drinkables. Either sweet and cold, or hot and savory, they provide a quick energy boost that will stay with you until lunch.

Steaming Breakfast Broth

4 Cups hot chicken or beef broth (soup base comes in handy here!)
1 Tablespoon dried parsley flakes **4 eggs**
1 teaspoon dried minced onion

Whirl the eggs in a blender until foamy. While still blending, slowly pour in the other ingredients. Pour into 4 mugs and top with a grating of homemade Parmesan cheese and a shake of paprika.

Fruitie Smoothie

1 Cup plain or vanilla yogurt (See Cheese/Dairy section)
1 Cup canned pineapple or any fruit of your choice
6-7 ice cubes **1 banana**
2 Tablespoons of sugar or honey **2 eggs,** optional

Whirl all the ingredients in a blender until smooth. Sprinkle with freshly grated nutmeg and garnish with a sprig of fresh mint for a frosty eye-opener. Serves two.

Main Dishes, Both Local and Distant

Here in the U. S. we have a wonderful diversity of cultures which have contributed to the melting pot nature of our national cooking pot. Everyone has a favorite ethnic food, and we hope with this section you will find yours and learn about some others. They all provide a means of varying the diet and providing new ways to use the standby staples you have stored. Though you may be feeding your family of four for as low as $10.00 a week, there is never any reason to feel bored doing so.!

Italian. . . Baked Cheese Manicotti

This dish is wonderful for preparing ahead and keeping in the freezer if company comes. All the cheese recipes are found in A Bite of Independence, keeping the cost of this dish to a minimum.

SAUCE:

1/3 Cup olive or vegetable oil
1 quart home canned tomatoes
1 Cup homemade tomato sauce
1 teaspoon dried oregano
1 teaspoon dried sweet basil
4 twists fresh ground pepper
1 Tablespoon sugar
1 teaspoon salt
2 Tablespoon parsley
1/4 teaspoon garlic powder
1 large onion, minced
1½ Cups water

MANICOTTI:

6 eggs
1½ Cups water
1½ Cups unbleached flour
1/4 teaspoon salt

FILLING:

4 Cups homemade cottage cheese
1 Cup diced homemade Mozzarella
1/2 Cup shredded Parmesan
4-5 twists fresh ground pepper
2 eggs, beaten
1 teaspoon salt
1½ Tablespoons parsley
Additional Parmesan for garnish

1. **First prepare the sauce:** Sauté the onion in the oil in a large pan. When translucent, add the rest of the ingredients. Mash the tomatoes with a fork, they should still be lumpy. Cover and simmer for one hour, stirring occasionally.

2. **While the sauce simmers**, make the manicotti: Warm the eggs to room temperature and combine all in a blender. Whirl just until smooth, then let set for 30 minutes. Preheat an 8 inch pan and spray with a nonstick spray. Quickly swirl about 3 Tablespoons of the batter over the bottom, tipping to coat evenly. Cook over medium heat just until the top is dry. Cool on a wire rack and stack with waxed paper separating the layers.

3. **Make the filling:** Combine all the ingredients, mixing well.

4. **Assemble:** Preheat oven to 350°. Pour a small amount of the sauce in the bottom of two 9″ x 13″ baking dishes. (If you desire to freeze one, line the pan with foil first.) Spread about 1/4 Cup of the filling across the center of a manicotti and roll it up. Place, seam side down, in the pan and continue until you have two layers. Cover with about 1 Cup of the remaining sauce and sprinkle with the additional Parmesan. Bake, uncovered, for 30 minutes. If freezing one, fold the foil over and freeze in the pan until solid. Remove from pan and label. To bake, return to the same sized pan, unwrapped and let thaw 1 hour. Bake, covered, about 45 minutes to 1 hour, or until bubbly in a 350° oven.

Good Old American Standby. . . Chili-Mac

1 Pound ground meat
or
2 Cups wheat meat hamburger
1½-2 Cups raw macaroni
1/4 teaspoon garlic powder
1 onion, chopped
2 Tablespoons chili powder
2-3 Cups home canned stewed or whole tomatoes
1 green pepper, chopped
1 Cup shredded homemade colby cheese

In a large skillet, brown the meat. Push to one side and sauté the onion in the drippings. (**Note**: If using **wheat meat,** hold it aside and instead, wilt the onion in a little vegetable oil, then proceed.) Stir in the green pepper, macaroni, tomatoes and chili powder and garlic powder. Cover, turn heat to low and cook until macaroni is tender and liquid absorbed. Add additional water or tomato if it appears too dry. Salt and pepper to taste, and stir in wheat meat, if using. Sprinkle with cheese, replace lid and remove from heat. Hold until cheese is melted and the wheat meat heated through. (**Note:** A cup of canned or frozen corn makes a colorful and tasty addition)

Italian. . . Lasagna

Another of the favorites at our seminars, this dish is sure to please your family as well. Another advantage is the fact that it freezes well, a sure boon to the busy homemaker or career minded.

16 homemade lasagna noodles (See index)
3 Cups homemade spaghetti sauce (See index)
1 Pound homemade colby cheese, shredded
1 Cup cooked corn
1/2 Cup Parmesan cheese
1/4 Cup chopped black olives
1/2 Cup wheat meat hamburger
Whole olives for garnish

In the bottom of a 9″ x 13″ baking dish, place a small layer of sauce. On top of this, place 4 cooked, drained lasagna noodles. Sprinkle with the wheat meat hamburger and some of the corn, shredded cheese, chopped olives, Parmesan and a little more sauce. Repeat, ending with four layers and the noodles on top. Pour the remaining sauce over and garnish with whole black olives. Bake in 350° oven 30 minutes, or until bubbly.

Pakistani. . . Whole Wheat Pilaf

While pilafs are generally considered as a side dish, the addition of some cut up leftover meat and a fresh garden salad can create a complete meal. If lacking the meat, cold hard boiled eggs, dusted with paprika, can be served on the side.

1/2 Cup chopped onion
1/4 Cup chopped celery
2 Cups cooked whole wheat berries (See Breakfast Section)
2 Cups chicken or beef bouillon, or reconstituted soup base
1 Tablespoon minced pimiento, for color (optional)
2 Tablespoons butter or margarine

Sauté onion and celery in the butter in a large skillet. When onion is golden, add wheat and stir briefly. Add bouillon and pimiento, cover and cook slowly until liquid is absorbed.

Saffron Rice

1/8 teaspoon crushed saffron threads
3/4 Cup raw rice
3/4 Cup hot water
1/4 teaspoon salt
2 Tablespoons margarine
1 3/4 Cups boiling water

In a heavy saucepan with tight fitting cover, dissolve the saffron threads in the 3/4 Cup hot water. To this add the rice and margarine. Next stir in the boiling water and salt. Cover and cook over lowest possible heat 25 to 30 minutes or until tender.

Indian. . . "Chicken" Curry and Saffron Rice

Known to be an expensive seasoning, saffron, in this case, is used in such a small amount that this recipe can still be called economical.

2 Tablespoons vegetable oil
1 Medium onion
1 teaspoon sugar
1½ Tablespoons cornstarch
1 Clove garlic
1 large tomato, chopped
3/4 teaspoon chicken soup base
3 Tablespoons raisins (optional)
2 Cup wheat meat chicken chunks (See index)
3/4 Cup milk, soy milk or Milk♥Lite®
2 Tablespoons homemade curry powder (See index)

In a large skillet, sauté the chopped onion and the minced garlic in the vegetable oil. Stir in the tomato, curry powder, sugar and soup base. Mix the cornstarch with the milk and add, stirring till smooth and thickened. Add the wheat meat chicken chunks and heat through. Add raisins for an authentic Indian flavor. Serve with saffron rice:

German. . . Hasenpfeffer (Braised Rabbit)

5-6 Pounds rabbit, cut up (1 large, or 2 small)
1 Tablespoon whole black peppercorns
6 Slices bacon scraps
1½ Cups homemade vinegar
1½ Cups water
4 Tablespoons sugar
1½ teaspoons salt
3 Whole cloves
1 Tablespoon flour
2 Medium onions, sliced
3 Carrots, sliced
2 Small bay leaves
3 stalks celery, sliced
1 Clove garlic, minced
1/8 teaspoon dried thyme
1/3 Cup sour cream

Combine the vinegar, water, sugar, salt, cloves, peppercorns, onions, carrots, bay leaves, celery, garlic, and thyme in a large bowl. Add the rabbit pieces and cover. Marinate in the refrigerator for two days, turning several times a day. Drain and dry the rabbit, reserving the marinade.

In a large skillet, fry the bacon until crisp. Set it aside and in the same pan, fry the rabbit which has been dredged in flour. When browned, add the reserved marinade and vegetables. Reduce the heat to low and simmer, covered, until the rabbit is tender. It could take about 1 hour for young rabbits, 1½ hours for older ones.

Remove the meat to a platter and keep warm while you prepare the sauce. From the marinade, remove the cloves and bay leaves. Blend in a blender until smooth, then return to the pan and stir in the sour cream which has been mixed with the flour. Heat just until thickened, stirring constantly. Add the reserved crumbled bacon and pour over the rabbit. Serve with boiled potatoes and cooked red cabbage for a traditional German dinner.

Southwestern U.S. - Burritos or Chimichangas

When eaten out of the hand, either steaming hot or cold, these are known as burritos. Crisp fry them and serve covered with hot red sauce and garnished with shredded cheese, sour cream, chopped tomato and lettuce, and you have chimichangas. . . one of the favorites at our seminars.

2 dozen homemade flour tortillas (See index)
3-4 Cups thinly sliced beef or chicken wheat meat roast (See index)
1 Cup red enchilada sauce (See index)
1 recipe thick green sauce (See index)
1 large onion, chopped
1 Pound homemade colby cheese, shredded
2-3 Cups additional red enchilada sauce
1 Head finely shredded lettuce
2 tomatoes, chopped
Sour Cream
Chopped black olives

Cut the sliced wheat meat roast into thin, matchstick pieces. Mix in a bowl with all the thick green sauce and 1 Cup of the red sauce. Set aside.

If the tortillas are too stiff to roll, soften them by placing between the folds of a clean damp towel and heat in the oven or microwave until soft and pliable.

TO ASSEMBLE: Take a tortilla, one at a time, from the towel and spread with a big spoonful of the filling along the bottom. Sprinkle a little cheese and onion on top and roll from the bottom, tucking the sides in as you roll. A little packet is thus made. Place, seam side down in a plastic bag until all have been rolled. To eat as **BURRITOS**, place in microwave or oven and heat until the cheese melts and then eat right away, or eat cold. To serve as **CHIMICHANGAS**, fry in about 1/2 inch hot oil until golden crisp. Place on serving plate and surround with finely shredded lettuce. Pour over a ladle of the extra red sauce, and on top of that, a sprinkling of extra shredded cheese and chopped tomatoes. Finish with a dollop of sour cream, over which is sprinkled a spoonful of chopped black olives for color contrast.

When serving, pass around additional heated red sauce. These freeze beautifully, either raw, or fried.

A

C

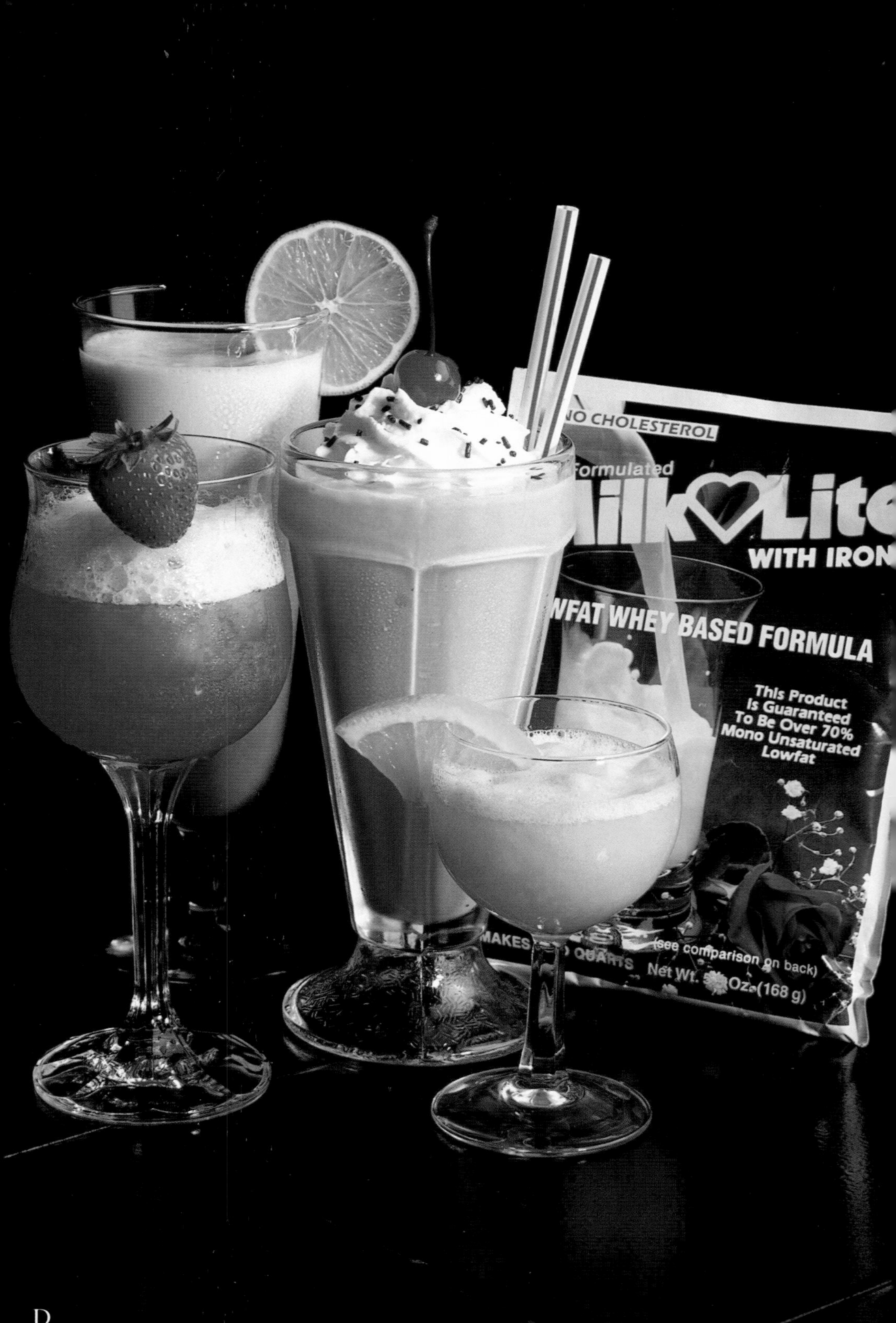
NO CHOLESTEROL
Formulated
ilk Lite
WITH IRON
WFAT WHEY BASED FORMULA
This Product
Is Guaranteed
To Be Over 70%
Mono Unsaturated
Lowfat
(see comparison on back)
Oz. (168 g)

D

Glorious Grains and Bountiful Beans

These next sections deal with the heart of your food storage. Unable to stand alone on our "$10.00 a week plan", grains and dry beans none-the-less form the backbone to permit all the variety and enjoyment the whole program brings.

It is the versatility of grains that surprises most people. Those who attend our seminars generally have an awareness of the value of wheat, the most well-known. We all love breads, crackers, pastries and pastas. But what astounds the majority, is wheat's ability to masquerade as meat. To most, this is a previously unheard of quality and is the factor in this program which makes the biggest impression.

Corn, we use in many ways as it forms the basis of many Mexican and Southwestern dishes, so popular nowadays.

Rice is a good substitute for potatoes and is one of the main food staples in many parts of the world.

There really cannot be enough said about the versatile soybean. In our program it is the perfect dairy substitute. For times when fresh fluid milk is unavailable, soybeans can always be found on the shelf.

The other grains and beans all shine in their own right and subsequent chapters and recipes are devoted to each. (You will find information on the proper storage of your dry grains and beans in the "Putting Aside" section.)

Please keep in mind that, versatile though they may be, these grains are all but part of the whole. Each part of this program is designed as an integral part of the others, which when practiced, really will enable you to "Feed a Family of Four For as Low as $10.00 a week."

Wheat: Bread, Crackers and Pasta

Wheat, the most widely cultivated food crop in the world, is often referred to as the Staff of Life, and with good reason. Its durability during storage, versatility, and nutrient value make it basic to any food storage program.

Whole grain wheat is one of the richest natural sources of vitamin B1, (thiamine), and it is also the source of other B complex vitamins, vitamin E, iron, copper, calcium, phosphorous, proteins, and carbohydrates.

Wheat comes to us in many forms and each is appreciated for its particular characteristics:

The Different Forms Of Wheat

Whole berries and cracked wheat, when cooked as a hot cereal or a pilaf, have a nutty goodness and impart the same nutty texture when added to breads.

Bread flour and some whole wheat flours are milled from hard wheat with a high gluten content. They are particularly suited to baking products with yeast, and for making **"wheat meat"**, a delicious meat substitute.

Durum wheat, another hard wheat with a high gluten level, is used commercially in the manufacture of pasta. (See section on Wheat Meat for discussion on gluten.)

Cake flour is milled from a soft wheat and is of very fine texture. It produces cakes with fine texture and tender crumb.

All-purpose flour serves most baking needs and is blended from both hard and soft wheats. It is also available in an unbleached form, retaining more of the nutrients that are ordinarily lost to white flour. While, for nutrition's sake, we generally prefer whole wheat flour (and when you grind your own that is exactly what you get); where white flour is called for, unbleached is the better choice. The results are imperceptible from white.

You will notice when grinding your own wheat that the flour, if undisturbed, falls into two distinct forms. One is of a very light texture, whereas the other appears quite a bit coarser. If carefully scooped from the pile, the lighter flour makes a fine pastry flour. There are also commercial whole wheat pastry flours on the market, milled from soft wheat, which can be purchased at some health food stores. These can be substituted for all purpose flour in cakes, cookies, and quickbreads.

Whole wheat flour contains wheat germ which is the nutrient-dense portion of the kernel. The fat which is found in the germ rapidly becomes rancid, so it is a good idea to grind only what you will use within a week. Any excess should be kept in the refrigerator or the freezer, warming to room temperature before using with yeast.

Why Whole Wheat?

While it is a known fact that whole wheat products are far superior to their white counterparts, the question is, why?

For some, accustomed to years of white flour, the switch to whole grains might prove difficult at first. But if one has an awareness of how foods interact within the body, it might help to cement the resolve.

As we know, refining the basic whole ground flour serves to remove the bran and the wheat germ. In the bran are found, in addition to fiber, carbohydrates, minerals, proteins, and vitamins. The germ contains almost all the nutritional resources to supply the growing seed, were it to sprout: vitamins B and E, iron and other minerals, polyunsaturated fats, protein, and carbohydrates. So, as you can see, refinement results in the loss of nearly half of wheat's nutritional value.

If this weren't sufficient cause for concern, consider: The body requires the nutrients lost to processing as essential for metabolizing the carbohydrates remaining in white flour. The body's only recourse then, is to pull these needed elements from within itself for proper digestion and assimilation. Therefore, not only is wheat's essential goodness lost, but the body is taxed as well when a diet relies predominantly upon white flour.

Bran is on everyone's mind these days and with good reason. It is essential for good digestion and bowel health that the ingested foods be moved swiftly and cleanly through the system. This is accomplished by peristalsis, or a rhythmic squeezing action, in the intestines and colon. Without the bran particles to provide the needed grip, the mass of material made gummy by white flour and its products fails to move cleanly, leaving behind a coating to coat and clog the colon.

This constipation and stagnation can lead to digestive upsets and possible disease as it encourages the proliferation of unhealthful micro-organisms. It is thought that colon and rectal cancer might be related to the development of carcinogenic secretions produced by some of these micro-organisms.

Other conditions associated with today's highly refined diet are thought to be linked to changes in the blood flow, brought on, in part, by changes in the intestinal rhythm. Hemorrhoids, coronaries, pulmonary embolus, varicose veins - these modern ills go hand in hand with the industrial world's refined diet.

A More Natural Lifestyle

When reviewed over the past 100 years or so, a pattern is seen to develop. As civilization and technology increased, the foods eaten were processed and further removed from their natural state. Correspondingly, the rate of degenerative diseases rose also. It is our feeling that a return to a more natural lifestyle, in not only the foods that we eat, but in our approach to living, as well, is essential for us to enjoy wholly this life we've been blessed with.

The approach to this whole book, therefore, is geared toward a back-to-basics, simpler and happier way of living. The reward is good health, a great economic boost, and a warm feeling of satisfaction.

Breads: Yeast

Since invented by the Egyptians over 5,000 years ago, yeast breads have been a staple on nearly every table.

Yeast and sourdough, (a wild form of yeast), are actually microscopic one-celled plants. They grow rapidly in a warm, moist environment, digesting sugar and releasing carbon dioxide as a by-product. It is this gas, trapped by the gluten framework, that causes the dough to rise.

As a rule, yeast is dissolved in water before being incorporated into the dough. The temperature is important for its growth is most active within the 105° - 115° range. If it is any cooler it grows too slowly; hotter, and the yeast cells die. The use of a thermometer is not essential to your success, for a few drops of the water dropped on the inside of your wrist should tell you the correct temperature. Just slightly warmer than lukewarm should be right.

Liquids Create The Character

A number of liquids can be used to make the dough. One tends first to think of water or milk. Water promotes a crispier crust and a wheatier flavor, while milk helps the bread to keep longer and adds nutrition plus a velvety crumb. It is not necessary to scald pasteurized milk, as it lacks the yeast-inhibiting enzyme found in raw milk. Actually, unless heating it to dissolve the sugar or melt the fat, it needs only to be heated to lukewarm. This saves considerable time as recipes usually say "scald and cool to lukewarm. . . "

Water in bread dough can be in several forms. A delicious addition is water remaining from cooking potatoes. The starches found in it and also in the water left from washing wheat meat help to form a light, beautiful loaf. The watery, protein-rich whey left from cheese making, buttermilk, soy milk and Milk♥Lite® are all interchangeable nutrition boosters and each adds a particular character to bread.

What else is needed?

The sugar needed for yeast growth is found naturally in the flour, or added in the form of white or brown sugar, honey, molasses, or even corn syrup. It aids in the browning and provides a delicious sweetness.

While salt is needed to bring out the other flavors, too much can have an inhibiting effect on the yeast. Without it, bread can taste a little flat. However, one of the advantages of home baking is the ability to leave it out if one is on a restricted diet.

Fat added to the dough, be it vegetable shortening, oil, butter, margarine or lard, lends it elasticity, permitting the leavening gas to expand freely. A crisp crust and added flavor also result from the addition of fat.

Eggs, where used, contribute flavor, color, and an even, fine texture. They heighten the nutrition and add richness to the bread.

General Hints For Successful Bread Baking

If there is any word of advice we would give to a beginning breadmaker, it would be **"RELAX!"** There really is no mystique to baking bread, nor does it have to consume your entire day, requiring undivided attention.

As long as you have an active yeast, and are careful not to get it too hot, bread dough can be very forgiving.

It used to be one could tell if a yeast was good by the foaming action when warm water was added. Today's yeast does not contain the extra starch that produced such foaming. To test, if in doubt, dissolve 1 Tablespoon yeast in 1/4 Cup warm water and add 1 teaspoon sugar. A live, active yeast should be foamy within 5 minutes.

Regarding flour, all the recipes in this section give an approximate amount of flour to use: the reason is flour differs in its ability to absorb moisture. This is due to varying protein and moisture content in flour and the conditions when you use it. The same recipe might call for more flour on a humid summer day than would be required in the winter, when the flour has had an opportunity to dry out in the cupboard.

A Little Goes A Long Way

So often bread's crumbly texture is directly related to the use of too much flour. We find that a "stiff dough" that is really easy to work with usually has too much flour, (the exception being French type bread, and that should be stiff). Keeping the dough slightly on the soft side makes it more difficult to work with, but a dough scraper helps with that problem. This is an invaluable tool in the kitchen, being merely a four or five inch flat dull metal blade with one side enclosed in a wooden grip. Lacking a dough scraper, a pancake turner should work about as well. Use the scraper to lift the sticky mass while kneading the final flour in prior to putting it in the bowl to rise.

Kneading dough is no time to be gentle. Do not be afraid to get in there and slam, punch, fold, turn and punch again. This helps to develop the gluten and distribute it throughout the dough. If you are kneading by hand it should take about 10 minutes. If you use a mixer with a dough hook, about five minutes should do it.

The next step, rising, gives you some leeway, time-wise. The dough should rise to twice its volume in the greased bowl and then be punched down to rise again. We have become occupied in other activities and totally forgotten about the dough rising, only to enter the kitchen and find it pouring over the edge of the bowl and all over the counter. This is where we speak of dough being forgiving, for it can be scooped up (the counter being clean) and returned to the bowl, getting punched down in the process. Each time you punch the dough down, the texture of the bread becomes more finely grained. we have punched dough four or five times with no ill results.

Now Is The Time to "Loaf"

Forming the loaves is a matter of turning the contents of the bowl onto a very lightly floured counter and chopping into approximately equal sized chunks. (You may prefer to use oil on the counter.) Flatten slightly with the hand, then grab each side and lift and slap, hard. Fold the sides in to approximately the size of the bread pan then slap it and fold it, lengthwise, into thirds, creasing the seams with the knuckles. It should now be about the size of the pan and, after shaping it up a little on the counter, it is ready to be placed in the greased pan. Sometimes, with a soft dough, the dough scraper is helpful to loosen and lift the loaf. Oil the top and cover with plastic to rise.

All the dough risings up to now have been doubling in size. Once the formed loaves are in the pan, it is important that they be watched closely for this time you want to catch them just before they double. Bread baked when it has risen too high tends to collapse in the oven, forming coarse textured, crumbly loaves with flat tops. Although you might find it difficult to do; turn the loaves out of the pan and reform them if you find them picture perfect, high and light before baking. Bear in mind that further rising takes place in the oven's heat.

We generally bake 12 to 14 loaves at a making, but the oven hold only six, "crowdedly". Covered with plastic, the remaining loaves wait their turn in the refrigerator where rising is retarded.

This brings to mind another time-saving tip: If you find time limited, preventing you from baking the same day, you can make the dough one day, and bake it the next. Simply double the amount of yeast, (yeasty flavor in bread is caused by too warm a rising area, not too much yeast), and refrigerate the dough. If chilled in the bowl, let the dough warm 2 hours before forming into loaves. If chilled in loaf pans, wait 10 minutes before putting into preheated oven.

Is It Bread Yet?

Bread is done when it produces a hollow sound when rapped on the bottom with the knuckles. If a white bread, it should be a golden brown on the bottom. If it seems heavy, or soggy, return to the oven - either in or out of the pan - for an additional 10 to 15 minutes and test again.

When done, remove from the oven and immediately take from the pans and place on wire racks to cool. If left, even for a minute, in the pan, the bottom gets soggy and the loaf loses its appeal. Some prefer to place the loaf on its side to cool, but we find less distortion if placed right side up.

In theory, homemade bread should be thoroughly cooled before slicing. Reality, being what it is, dictates that one loaf be sacrificed the minute it no longer burns your fingers. What is lost in texture is gained in the flavor of a fresh, hot slice oozing with butter and honey. (Heating the knife helps to cut it a little easier.)

Happy baking with these recipes. Each one is a proven favorite of ours and sure to become yours also. Relax and enjoy; you'll never buy "store bought" again.

Dough Enricher

A whole wheat loaf is characteristically a heavier and more dense loaf than white. Some authorities suggest that the sharp bran particles in the flour cut the gluten strands, weakening the frame work. Others reply that whole grain flour inherently lacks the quantity of gluten found in white, leading to a more compact loaf.

Whatever the case, the texture of a whole grain loaf is greatly improved, with no change in taste, by the addition of a dough enricher. It contains the same natural ingredients, not preservatives, that commercial bakeries use to lighten their loaves of whole grain bread. Try it, and see if you don't notice the improvement.

Dough Enricher (Continued)

1/4 Cup soy flour (See index)
3/4 Cup cornstarch
3/4 -1 Cup gluten flour*
2 - 3 teaspoons lecithin granules*
1 Tablespoon dry yeast
4 Tablespoons sugar
1 Cup whey powder*
7 Vitamin C tablets, crushed

* Available at health food stores

Mix together and store in an airtight jar. To use, add 1 Tablespoon per loaf in your favorite recipe. Add with the first addition of flour.

Yeast

There are many good commercial yeasts available in anything from one tablespoon size packets to five pound sacks or more. Sometimes, however, it is fun to try your own. Here are a couple of recipes:

Everlasting Yeast

2 small peeled potatoes
2 teaspoons sugar
1 Tablespoon dry yeast
4½ Cups potato water
3/4 teaspoon salt

Boil potatoes in water until soft. Drain and reserve the water. Mash potatoes, add the sugar and salt. Let cool. Measure the reserved water, add more if necessary to make 4½ Cups. Mix the warm water, potato mixture and yeast together. Cover loosely and set aside in a warm place to ferment. When bubbling action has ceased, store, covered, in the refrigerator. Use 2 Cups of this liquid yeast to replace 2 Cups of liquid and the yeast in a 4 loaf yield recipe. Remove from the refrigerator the night before you intend to use it so it can warm up to room temperature and be ready to use.

Yeast Cakes (Hops)

2 Tablespoons sugar
4 Cups cornmea
1½ Cups potato water
1 Cup dried hops (available at health food stores)
1 Cup mashed potatoes
1 package dried yeast

Simmer the hops for one minute with water to barely cover. Strain and reserve the water. Dissolve the yeast in the warm potato water and add the sugar. Mix well and stir in the mashed potatoes. Stir in the flour till no lumps remain and then add sufficient reserved hops water to make a medium-soft dough. Let rise until doubled. Punch down and add cornmeal to make a stiff dough. Roll out on a board to 1/2 inch thickness and cut into 2″ cakes. Let air dry, turning frequently. Store in a dry place for use within 6 months. To use, crumble one cake into 2 Cups of warm water with 1 teaspoon sugar. Add a little flour and let it become active before adding to the dough.

Basque Sheepherder Bread

Originating in the Basque Province of northern Spain, this bread, traditionally baked in a cast iron dutch oven, has become one of our most popular requests.

13 1/2 Cups flour
3/4 Cup soft butter or margarine
3 teaspoons salt
3 Tablespoons <u>or</u> 3 packages dried yeast
Butter flavored shortening or margarine for greasing pans
5 Cups warm water
1/2 Cup sugar

Put the soft butter or margarine in a large mixing bowl with the sugar and salt. Stir in the warm water, then sprinkle the yeast over surface. Let wait a couple of minutes to soften, then stir until dissolved. The butter does not have to melt. Beat in the flour, adding gradually toward the last. Keep slightly on the sticky side. Turn out on lightly floured board and knead, adding flour if necessary. Put dough in an oiled bowl, turn over to bring the oiled side up and cover with plastic wrap. Let rise until doubled. Punch down and turn out on oiled counter. Cut in half and round each half into a ball. Thickly spread the margarine, or the butter flavored shortening around the inside of two 10″ cast iron dutch ovens. (This is what gives the loaves their typically crunchy crust) Put the balls of dough in the pans, oil the tops and cover with plastic. Put into 375° oven when the loaves have risen about 1 inch above the tops. Bake 40 to 45 minutes until they are a rich deep golden brown and sound hollow when tapped. Using two pot holders, carefully lift out of the pans and place on wire racks to cool. Makes two very large loaves, and freezes well.

Homemade Hamburger or Hot Dog Buns

This recipe calls for lard, and although any other fat can be substituted, the distinctive flavor that sets these rolls apart from others will be changed.

10-11 Cups flour (Use half whole wheat, if desired)
2 Cups milk, soy milk or Milk♥Lite®
3/4 Cup sugar
2/3 Cup lard
1 egg beaten with 2 Tablespoons water
2 Tablespoons <u>or</u> 2 packages dried yeast
Sesame seeds, optional
2 teaspoons sugar
1 Cup warm water
3 teaspoons salt
2 eggs

Put 3/4 Cup sugar, lard, salt and milk in saucepan. Heat until lard melts, stirring to dissolve sugar. Let cool till lukewarm. In a large mixing bowl dissolve the yeast with the 2 teaspoons sugar and water. Let stand about 5 minutes, then add the warm milk mixture. Beat in 5 Cups of flour then add the eggs and beat again until smooth. Add enough flour to make a very soft dough. With the aid of the dough scraper and using a minimum of flour, knead about 8 to 10 minutes. Lift, (it will be a very slack dough) and place in oiled bowl, turning over to coat surface. Cover and let rise until doubled, about 1 hour. Punch down, let rest 10 minutes and working with 1/2 of the dough at a time, roll out on floured counter top to 1/2″ thickness. Cut, close together, with a floured large tuna can, both ends removed. Knead the scraps together into a ball, flatten and cut again. Repeat with the other half of dough. You should be able to get almost 36. Place on greased baking sheets, brush tops with an egg, beaten with 2 Tablespoons of water. Sprinkle with sesame seeds, if desired. Cover, let rise till almost doubled. Bake at 350° 15 to 18 minutes or until golden. Remove to wire racks to cool. When cool, split with sharp knife and put in plastic bags. The secret to having these buns soft like store-bought is to keep the dough very soft.

For hot dog buns:

Roll out as for hamburger buns, but cut into 4″ x 1″strips. (It is handy to use a pizza wheel, if you have one.) Roll each into about a 5 1/2″ bun. Place on greased sheet and flatten slightly with your palm. Cover, let rise until almost double, bake as above.

French Baguettes

Another oft requested recipe is for French bread. While these are baked in a special baguette pan - giving them their traditional cylindrical shape - they can be baked on a cookie sheet where they assume a flatter, though no less delicious form.

2 3/4 Cups warm water
1 Tablespoon or package dry yeast
1 egg beaten with 2 Tablespoons water
Sesame seeds, or poppy seeds, if desired
2 1/2 Tablespoons sugar
1 Tablespoon salt
7 Cups flour

Stir the yeast, salt, sugar and water together until dissolved. Add about 6 Cups flour, stirring as best you can. It will be a shaggy mass. Put about 1 Cup flour on the kneading counter and place the dough on it and knead 8 to 10 minutes, adding flour if necessary. This dough you want stiff. When smooth and satiny, place in greased bowl, turning over to grease the top. Cover and let rise until doubled. Punch down, turn onto oiled counter, cut into 1/4ths. With hands, flatten into an oblong. Beginning lengthwise, fold into thirds, tucking the sides in about half way through. Crease seam with knuckles, roll back and forth to smooth up and place on greased baking sheets or in greased baguette pans. With scissors, snip the loaf diagonally at 3 to 4 inch intervals. Brush the loaves with an egg wash, (1 egg, beaten with 2 Tablespoons water) and sprinkle with seeds, if desired. Cover and let rise until doubled. Bake in preheated 450° oven for 15 minutes, then turn down to 350° and bake for an additional 30 minutes. Cool on wire racks.

These freeze beautifully if wrapped tightly in foil. To re-crisp, put the foil wrapped loaves in the 350° oven for twenty minutes. Unwrap and let cool on a wire rack. (They make good garlic bread, and submarine sandwiches!) Makes 4 crispy loaves.

Orange-Flecked Raisin Bread

Be careful, this bread can quickly make you an addict. It is delicious spread with homemade cream cheese which has been mixed with a little orange juice and grated rind.

6 Cups milk, soy milk or Milk♥Lite®
3 Tablespoons or packages dry yeast
3/4 Cup lard or vegetable shortening
4 Tablespoons grated orange rind
2 beaten eggs (optional)
3/4 Cup warm water
1 Cup sugar
18 Cups flour
6 teaspoons salt
4-5 Cups raisins

In a saucepan, heat the milk, sugar, salt and shortening. Add the raisins. In a separate bowl, combine the yeast with the warm water, let stand until softened, about 10 minutes. Mix the two together in a large mixing bowl, taking care the milk mixture is just warm.

Beat in about 6 Cups flour, beating well. Add the orange rind and beaten eggs. Mix well. Stir in the remainder of the flour to make a dough that is moderately stiff, yet still a little sticky. Turn out on lightly floured board and knead 8 to 10 minutes, adding flour sparingly as needed.

Place in oiled bowl, turning to coat the top. Cover and let rise until doubled. Punch down and let rise again. Turn out on lightly floured counter and divide into 6 equal pieces. Let rest, covered, for 10 minutes.

Flatten into an oblong the width being the size of the pan. Roll up tightly, sealing the seam with your knuckles. Place in greased pans, seam side down. Cover and let rise until almost double. Then bake in 375° oven for 30 minutes, or until golden brown and hollow sounding when rapped on the bottom with your knuckles. Remove to wire racks to cool; frost with a little powdered sugar mixed with water to make a thick drizzle. Drizzle back and forth across the loaves in a zigzag pattern. Makes 6 loaves.

* **Variation:** For cinnamon bread, omit the raisins and spread the dough with soft butter or margarine before rolling it up. On top of that, evenly crumble brown sugar, then sprinkle with cinnamon. Roll up tightly and bake as above.

Basic White, Oatmeal or Cracked Wheat Bread

4 Cups milk, soy milk or Milk♥Lite®
3/4 Cup sugar or honey
1 1/2 Cubes margarine
4 Tablespoons or packages dry yeast
24 Cups flour
4 Cups warm water
8 teaspoons salt

Heat margarine, sugar, salt and milk together in saucepan. In small bowl dissolve the yeast in one cup of the warm water. Pour the milk mixture into a large mixing bowl and add the remaining 3 Cups water. (Add cold water if you find that the milk mixture is not cooled sufficiently to risk adding the yeast.) Add the dissolved yeast and beat in enough flour to make a moderately soft dough. Turn out on floured counter top and knead 8 to 10 minutes, adding flour if needed. Place in oiled bowl, turn over to oil top, cover with plastic and let rise in a warm place until doubled. Punch down, let rise again. Turn out on lightly floured counter and divide into 6 equal pieces. Let rest 5 to 10 minutes, then form into loaves. Place in greased loaf pans, let rise almost double. Bake in 375° oven 30 minutes or until golden brown and hollow sounding on the bottom when rapped with the knuckles. Yields 6 loaves.

* **For oatmeal bread**, replace 1/4 Cup of the sugar with molasses, and add 2 - 3 Cups dry rolled oats with the flour. Before baking, brush the tops of the loaves with an egg beaten with 2 Tablespoons of water and sprinkle a few dry rolled oats on the surface.

* **For cracked wheat**, add 2 Cups cooled, cooked cracked wheat before adding flour.

* **If desired**, a third of the flour may be replaced with whole wheat flour for a mild, light wheat loaf.

Dutch Crunch Topping

A bakery from my childhood stands out in my memory for its delicious Dutch crunch loaf. The tops of the loaves were deep golden brown with jagged fissures of white cracking the crust. The appearance was striking and the texture marvelously crunchy. Here is the recipe; try it on any of your favorite bread recipes.

2 1/2 Cups rice flour*
1 1/2 Cups warm water
3 Tablespoons or packages dry yeast
4 1/2 teaspoons salt
2 Tablespoons vegetable oil
6 teaspoons sugar

* Run rice through mill on fine grind

Sprinkle yeast over the warm water. Add remaining ingredients when yeast is dissolved and beat well. Just before baking spread the mixture on the surface of the risen loaves. Bake as usual.

Pizza Dough

$3^1/_2$ Cups flour, unbleached or whole wheat
1 Tablespoon or package dry yeast
2 Tablespoons olive oil
1 Cup warm water
1 teaspoon sugar
$1^1/_2$ teaspoons salt

Mix sugar, yeast, and water until yeast is dissolved. Add salt and olive oil. Beat in flour and knead until soft and elastic. Put in oiled bowl, turning over to oil surface. Cover and let rise until doubled, about 45 minutes. Punch down and divide in half. Let rest, covered 10 minutes. (This permits the dough to relax so you can roll it out easier) Roll into a circle to fit the pizza pan, or cookie sheet. Lift into pizza pan (generously oiled with olive oil) and pat to fit. Top with favorite sauce and toppings. Bake 450° - 475° for 20 to 25 minutes on lowest oven rack. (Another delicious crust can be made using the Baguette recipe.)

100% Whole Wheat Bread

With the use of the dough enricher (See recipe given in this section) this bread comes out unbelievably light textured. It has all the goodness and flavor that only whole wheat can deliver. It makes excellent toast.

$2^1/_2$ Tablespoons dry yeast
$5^1/_2$ Cups warm water
2/3 Cup honey or sugar
12 Cups whole wheat flour
1/2 Cup vegetable oil
$1^1/_2$ Tablespoons salt

Dissolve yeast in warm water. stir in oil and honey or sugar and salt. Stir until mixed. Beat in the dough enricher and the flour. Turn out on oiled counter and knead until smooth and elastic. Divide into four equal pieces. Form into loaves and place in oiled pans. Cover and let rise almost double then bake in a 375° oven 30 minutes or until loaves sound hollow when rapped on the bottom. Yield: 4 loaves.

"Free-for-nothing 'Coffee'"

1 slice black, burnt toast (old heels are good for this)
2 Cups boiling water
1/4 teaspoon chicory

Break toast into a pan, add chicory. Cover with boiling water and let steep 2 to 3 minutes. Strain and serve. Makes 2 cups.

Breads: Quick

Up until the mid 1800's, housewives had relatively limited methods of leavening their baked goods. They used "starters", or "emptyings" as they were called in some regions, for their bread. Air leavened some things with the beating of egg whites, and steam was used in raising items like popovers. "Saleratus", the name in use at the time for baking soda, was found on many a kitchen shelf.

For the housewife of that era, these methods had various drawbacks. Starters required lengthy sponge development and kneading, eggs were not always plentiful, and steam was limiting. Saleratus required the mixing with an acid such as found in sour milk, molasses, buttermilk, lemon juice, or vinegar to generate its leavening carbon dioxide and the use of soda required then, as it still does today, speed from mixing to the oven before the leavening action was lost.

The Birth of Baking Powder

During the 1850's the discovery was made that soda could be mixed with an acid in the dry form, not to be activated until moistened. Although still requiring speedy, yet gentle, handling, it permitted greater flexibility in ingredients and thus baking powder was born.

Further refinements produced a powder that not only began working when moistened, but continued to work from the heat of the oven, and so, double-acting baking powder came into being.

Initially viewed with suspicion, (for many thought baking powder inhibited the sex-drive!), it nonetheless gained acceptance and a widespread following for the new, quick and reliable style of baking it permitted.

Quick Bread Tips

Today we have a wealth of recipes for last-minute hurry-ups; delicious bread, muffins and biscuits with baking powder or soda at their base.

Just as yeast and soda/baking powder differ in their means of producing carbon dioxide - (yeast being the result of a living organism's growth, while the other is strictly a chemical reaction) - so yeast breads and quick breads require different handling techniques:

- Mix dry ingredients together first, and unless otherwise directed, mix the soda or baking powder in with the dry ingredients so it is evenly distributed throughout the dough. Brown spots and a bitter flavor can result from an uneven mixing.

- Add the liquid all at once and stir just until moistened. Avoid overmixing, for lumpy batter is typical of quick breads. Any attempt to mix it smooth generally results in a tough product filled with tunnels.
- For recipes requiring creaming sugar and butter together, add the flour alternately with the milk, beginning and ending with the flour to prevent curdling.
- Do not worry about brown sugar lumps. They simply melt in the baking to become little dark spots of sweet caramel.
- If adding nuts or fruits, coat them with flour first to prevent their sinking to the bottom of the batter.
- Have the oven preheated when using soda; you want to bake it while the dough or batter is still light and airy. By the same token, mix gently.
- When cutting biscuits, do not twist the cutter. This crimp-seals the edges, thus preventing them from rising as high as they might.
- Do not thump to determine doneness. Use a clean broomstraw, cake tester or toothpick inserted in the middle. If any moist particles adhere, bake a little longer.
- After removal from the oven, leave in the pan about 10 minutes to firm up. It won't be so likely to crumble when cut.

Types of Baking Powder

We have available to us today, three types of baking powder. They are: **1. DOUBLE ACTING**, (Clabber Girl, Calumet, and Crescent);**2. PHOSPHATE**, (Rumford, Dr. Price); and **3. TARTRATE**, (Swansdown, Royal).

The recipes in this book call for double acting powder, but if you need to adjust for a different type, the conversions are: 2 1/2 teaspoons Phosphate or 3 teaspoons Tartrate for every 2 teaspoons of double acting baking powder called for.

Homemade Baking Powder

You can make your own baking powder by combining 2 parts cream of tartar with 1 part cornstarch and 1 part soda. This is a single acting powder and will require 2 teaspoons for every 1 teaspoon in the recipe. With this powder be sure to have the oven preheated and bake immediately after mixing.

In this section are a few of our favorite Quick Breads, including Waffles, Pancakes, Biscuits, and even Flour Tortillas.

Oat N' Wheat Waffles

These are so easy to make and so healthful for you. They are best if made in a Belgian Waffle Iron, for its deep valleys can hold the sweetened fruit or nuts that go so well with this treat.

3/4 Cup rolled oats*
1 Cup whole wheat berries*
2 teaspoons baking powder
3/4 teaspoon salt
3 eggs, separated
1/4 Cup vegetable oil
1 3/4 Cup milk, soy milk, Milk♥Lite® or water

* Put both through the mill on fine grind

In a large bowl, mix the dry ingredients. Combine egg yolks, (beaten), oil and milk or water. Stir in the dry ingredients. Beat egg whites stiff and gently fold in. Bake in preheated waffle iron until golden crisp, about 4 minutes. Serve hot with sweetened fruit or syrup. Makes about 5 to 6 waffles.

Whole Wheat Blender Pancakes

This recipe is a good one to introduce children to whole grain goodness. They love the flavor, not realizing how good it is for them. I speak from experience: The recipe is from my father.

1/2 Cup whole wheat berries
1 1/8 Cup milk or buttermilk
1/2 Cup water
3 eggs, separated
2 Tablespoons honey
1/4 Cup unbleached flour
1/4 teaspoon each, salt and soda
1 Tablespoons melted butter or margarine

At least 12 hours before making this recipe, soak the wheat in the 1/2 Cup water. when ready to use, drain and rinse. Put in blender with milk or buttermilk and blend for 5 minutes. In a separate bowl, beat the egg whites until stiff. To the blender add the remaining ingredients excepting the whites. Blend for 1 more minute, then transfer to a larger bowl and fold in the egg whites. Bake on a hot griddle, watching carefully as they brown quickly.

Flaky Buttermilk Biscuits

The secret to making these flaky layers is to cut the fat in to where it is the size of large peas. The best flavor is provided by using lard, but in the interest of health, we nowadays use vegetable shortening. Resist the temptation to cut it in finely.

4 Cups unbleached flour
1/3 Cup vegetable shortening
4 teaspoons baking powder
1/3 Cup lard or veg. shortening
1 teaspoon soda
1 1/2 Cups buttermilk
1 teaspoon salt

Flaky Buttermilk Biscuits (Continued)

Sift the dry ingredients together. With a pastry blender, or two knives, cut the first 1/3 Cup of shortening in until it resembles coarse cornmeal. Then cut the second 1/3 Cup shortening or lard in until it is the size of large peas. With a fork, stir in the buttermilk, all at once, mixing only until the flour is moistened. Knead very gently, about 30 seconds, and roll out to a 3/4 inch thickness. Cut with floured biscuit cutter, taking care not to twist the cutter. Place in a greased baking pan - close together for soft biscuits, 1/2 inch apart for crispy sided ones. Brush or dip the tops in melted butter or margarine, then bake in a hot oven, 475° for 12 to 15 minutes.

"On-Hand" Bran Muffins

Keep a covered jar of this batter in the refrigerator for up to two weeks and you can have a healthful hot muffin at a moment's notice.

3 Cups whole bran cereal
1 Cup boiling water
2 Cups buttermilk
2 1/2 teaspoons salt
1/2 teaspoon baking soda
3/4 Cup raisins or chopped prunes
3 small eggs, beaten
1/2 Cup vegetable oil
1 Cup sugar
2 1/2 Cups unbleached flour

Put the bran cereal in a large bowl and over it pour the boiling water. Stir and let cool before adding the eggs, buttermilk and oil, Blend well and add fruit. Stir the dry ingredients together then stir into the bran mixture. Refrigerate, covered, or spoon into paper lined muffin pans. Bake at 425° for about 20 minutes, or until the tops are firm. Makes 2 to 2 1/2 dozen.

Flour Tortillas

Having no leavening at all makes it difficult to classify this as a quick bread. A popular bread of the Sonoran state of Mexico, (where they are served hot at the table, covered with a damp napkin), these tortillas find their use in many of the dishes we love here. Unlike some tortillas which are thick and puffy, these are best when made as thin as you can stretch and roll them.

6 Cups unbleached flour
3 teaspoons salt
3/4 Cup vegetable shortening
1 1/2 Cups lukewarm water

In a large mixing bowl, stir the flour and salt. Add shortening and cut in well with pastry blender. Stir in the lukewarm water and mix well. Knead on lightly floured counter top about 50 times. Divide into 18 equal pieces and form each into a ball. Cover with a damp cloth or plastic and let rest for 10 minutes.

Keeping the others covered while you work, take a ball of dough and flatten and stretch it until it reaches about 5 inches across. Place on a clean, unfloured counter top and roll with a rolling pin from the center outward. Periodically lift and stretch the edges, following with a rolling to "lock the stretch in place". If a hole should develop, wet the margins with a little water and roll a patch in place. Lift off carefully and place on a large ungreased griddle over medium heat.

Cook until golden brown in spots, taking care not to break the air bubbles that form. Turn once. Serve warm, buttered as bread, or to make burritos, chimichangas, quesadillas, or Olé Apple Strudels, (See the index for above recipes.)

Crackers

Until learning to make our own, crackers were one item on the grocery list that was considered expendable. Granted, they were delicious as an accompaniment to soups and chili, were great as a snack item, but hardly justifiable when considered how rapidly they were consumed. Now, with these easy recipes, delicious, crispy fresh preservative-free crackers of all varieties are within easy reach. With a little experimenting, you can have flavors and shapes the stores never thought of. My children love to make their own and, with the cost for commercial, I'm happy to let them!

Buttery Thins

These taste similar to those little round ones those famous elves are known for. Although the flavor is best when made with real butter, for those lacking a cow the expense is less with margarine.

4 Cups unbleached flour
1 Cup chilled butter or margarine
3/4 Cup milk, soy milk or Milk♥Lite®
1/2 teaspoons baking soda
1/2 teaspoon salt
1 Tablespoon vinegar

With pastry blender or two knives, cut the butter into the flour until the size of peas. Stir the remaining ingredients together and with a fork, gently mix into the flour mixture. Press into a ball and chill for 5 to 10 minutes. Break off a piece about the size of a tennis ball and place in the center of a flat cookie sheet coated with nonstick spray. Place a sheet of waxed paper on top and roll it out, directly on the baking sheet until it is covered evenly. You will find unincorporated pieces of butter showing, but that is fine. It is what contributes to the flakiness. Gently peel off the waxed paper and cut with a pastry wheel or knife into diamonds, squares, etc. Prick surface with a fork and place in a preheated 375° oven for 20 minutes. Watch carefully as the margins tend to brown first. You may need to remove them first and continue to bake the centers. If they are underdone, they will be chewy instead of crisp. Salt immediately after removing from the oven. Store in an airtight jar, (if there are any left!).

Wheaty Thins

1/2 Cup whole wheat flour
1/2 Cup white flour
1/2 teaspoon salt
1/4 Cup milk, soy milk or Milk♥Lite®
1 Tablespoon wheat germ
1/4 Cup vegetable oil
1 teaspoon molasses

Mix dry ingredients in a large bowl. Combine the remaining ingredients and proceed as with the Buttery Thins recipe. Bake 20 minutes at 350°, taking care they do not get too brown. Salt while hot. Store in an airtight jar.

Graham Crackers

1½ Cups unbleached flour
3/4 Cup whole wheat flour
1/2 teaspoon salt
3 Tablespoons water
1/3 Cup brown sugar
1/4 Cup butter or margarine
1/3 Cup honey
Cinnamon/sugar (optional)

In a medium sized bowl, combine all the dry ingredients except the cinnamon and sugar. Cut in the margarine to the texture of cornmeal. Stir together the honey and water and mix well with the dry ingredients. Divide in half and roll each half out on an ungreased cookie sheet to 1/4″ thickness. Cut into desired shapes and prick with a fork and sprinkle with cinnamon and sugar, if desired. Bake in a 375° oven for approximately 10 minutes. Store in an airtight container when cool.

Pasta

No longer the "Whipping Boy" of nutritionalists, pastas have finally come of age. Recognized as a source of the complex carbohydrates the body needs to function properly, spaghetti, macaroni, noodles… all have shed their guilty images, and we pasta lovers have come out of hiding. It is nice to know that something so easy to make, so inexpensive and filling, is actually so good for you! That cannot be said about too many things these days.

Glancing through a pasta book, one tends to be overwhelmed at the myriad of names. While there seems to be an untold number of kinds, it all is derived from essentially one basic dough. Being a very malleable dough, it is formed in a number of different shapes, hence the number of different names. Different vegetable pureés can be added to provide color interest and a subtle change in flavor.

If pasta can be described in one word, it is **FUN**. It is fun to look at, fun to make, fun to eat, and, in the dry state, makes fun decorations and ornaments.

Here are the directions for making this most versatile food, and some of our favorite recipes. **Have fun!**

Pasta I (Good for Ravioli)

3-4 Cups unbleached or whole wheat flour
4 large eggs
1/2 Cup water
pinch of salt

Beat together the eggs, water and salt. Add enough flour to make a firm, compact dough. Knead. Divide in half and while keeping one half covered, roll out the other as thin as possible. If making noodles, cut into strips with pizza cutter, pastry wheel, or sharp knife. Either cook in salted boiling water and serve, or dry and store in glass jars or plastic bags. Can be frozen also.

For ravioli: Divide in half. Roll as thin as possible. Place a spoonful of prepared filling about every two inches over the surface of the pasta. On top of this lay another sheet of pasta, previously rolled out. Cut with pizza wheel or sharp knife midway between filling. Seal the edges of each ravioli with fork and either freeze, or boil gently for 10 minutes in salted water. Drain and serve with your favorite spaghetti sauce. **(See index)**

Cheese Filling:

2 Cups homemade cottage cheese
2 eggs, beaten
1 Tablespoon parsley
1/4 teaspoon salt
1/3 Cup grated homemade Parmesan

Wheat Meat Filling:

1/3 Cup minced onion
1 stalk of celery, chopped fine
1 Tablespoon margarine
1½ Cups homemade tomato sauce
2 Tablespoon brown sugar
1/4 teaspoon dry mustard
2 Cups wheat meat hamburger

In medium saucepan sauté the onion and celery in the margarine until wilted. add the remaining ingredients except the wheat meat. Heat through, then add the wheat meat. Use to fill the ravioli.

Basic Pasta II

$3^1/_2$ Cups flour, either whole wheat or unbleached
5 large eggs, beaten
2 Tablespoons oil
4 - 6 Tablespoons water

Put the flour in a medium bowl and make a well in the center. Into this pour the liquid ingredients. Mix the flour in from the sides until a stiff dough is formed. Knead briefly.

BY HAND: Roll out on a floured surface until very thin, about 1/16 inch thick. Dust with flour and let dry a minute or two then roll up as for a jelly roll. Slice in the desired width. These can be cooked right away in salted water, dried, or frozen. If frozen, they do not need to thaw before cooking.

BY MANUAL PASTA MACHINE: Feed through the rollers several times until smooth and elastic. Flour lightly if it feels tacky. Put through successively thinner settings until desired thickness is reached. Cut into desired shapes.

BY ELECTRIC PASTA MAKER: Mix dough with wire whip or dough hook until it resembles small popcorn. It should look somewhat dry, but if too dry, add a little water. Feed into the hopper with the desired attachment, be it macaroni, spaghetti, shells, etc. Many more shapes are possible with this type of machine. The pasta may be cooked in boiling, salted water, dried or frozen.

To Make Flavored, Colored Pasta

Make pasta as above, replacing water with:

1. Puréed spinach for green,
2. Puréed tomato for orange,
3. Puréed beets for red.

Chinese Noodles (Chow Mein Noodles)

Make pasta, above, and use the spaghetti attachment. Cut in approximately 1″ lengths. Fry in hot oil until golden brown and crisp. Store in an airtight container.

Wheat Meat. . .

An Exciting Alternative to Meat

. . .At An Exciting Price!

Very well the most important chapter in this book, this is where the magic lies, where the whole concept comes to life. As in motion picture magic where there is a star and a cast of supporting characters, so it is here with wheat meat; all the other chapters serve to lend support and variety.

It is difficult not to get excited, for in these days of escalating super-market prices, the budget finds itself being squeezed tighter and tighter. A great deal of this squeeze is exerted by the high price of meat. Although we show you ways to save on your meat bill by raising your own, we are certainly aware that not everyone has the facilities, nor inclination to do so. That, coupled with the fact that there is a great segment of the population who, for various reasons abstains from meat, leads us into the discussion of wheat meat. The greater bulk of our mail comes from people asking about wheat meat: What is it, How is it made, How does one serve it?

Wheat meat, simply stated, is gluten, formed and flavored to where it is nearly indistinguishable from real meat. Gluten is derived from proteins found almost exclusively in wheat, and when kneaded with water they form an insoluble, elastic material. This is the same framework that traps carbon dioxide bubbles, causing bread to rise.

Can Something Taste Good And Be Good for You?

A meal with wheat meat as its core can satisfy the hunger for meat. This is demonstrated by people's responses at our seminars: No one realizes until told, after the fact, that the meatballs in their spaghetti were not really meat, that the roast chicken with dressing and gravy never saw a barnyard, that the shrimp never contained a grit of sand, that the lunchmeat was actually GOOD for you, the list goes on and on. . .

Wheat meat contains no cholesterol, and has **1/3** fewer calories than hamburger. Lacking the amino acid, lysine, is the only thing that prevents wheat meat from being considered a complete protein. This is easily compensated for by the manner in which it is prepared and served, for lysine is found in eggs, beans, soy products, Brewer's yeast, dairy products and nuts.

As you can surmise, meals with wheat meat are economical. It takes only two pounds of wheat flour to produce 1¼ pounds of wheat meat. You can see where fantastic savings can result if you are able to purchase your wheat in bulk. Not much is needed in the way of equipment. If you purchase wheat berries you will need a grain mill; other than that all you need is a meat grinder or food processor, large bowl or dishpan, and a colander.

The investment in time is also minimal. When we state that our plan is easier and quicker than going to the store, we are also considering the preparation time involved. It takes no more than 20-25 minutes to make about 8 pounds of wheat meat, the raw material from which many meals can be made.

In this chapter we will show you how to make the basic "meats" such as ground beef, beef and pork roasts, ham, chicken roasts and nuggets, shrimp; all meats with which you are already familiar. We will provide recipes using these meats, and once you master a few ground rules, (for techniques can vary from those using real meat), you will be able to substitute freely in your own favorite recipes. There is nothing you cannot do with wheat meat that you cannot do with real meat.

A considerable amount of the magic - or delightful deception - of wheat meat is found in the use of sauces. The mind is programmed to expect certain flavors and textures from particular dishes and the right sauce or gravy aids the palate in the deception. A selection of our favorite sauces can be found in the **"Bind It Together or Dress It Up"** section.

Soup base is essential to the illusion of meat. Many commercial brands are available or you may make your own. See **"Leftover"** section for aid in locating sources, or for the homemade recipe.

Some Tricks To Get The Treat

Wheat meat should never be overcooked. As with Cinderella whose magic was lost when she overstayed her allotted time, so it is with wheat meat: over cook wheat meat, and you end up with toast. This is why, in most cases, it is added toward the last. Wheat meat's affinity for liquids is another reason it is generally the last added ingredient. If cooked in liquids in the traditional manner of true meats, it loses its meat-like texture and becomes soggy.

If, when baking the gluten, (the precursor to wheat meat), you feel it may have overcooked, try placing it in a plastic bag for a few minutes. Often that is all it takes to restore it to a proper texture. The converse holds true; wheat meat that is too soft to taste "meaty" can be improved by placing it on a greased cookie sheet in a 300°-350° oven for a few minutes to half an hour. The time and temperature depend upon the size, and whether sliced or whole.

Some of our recipes using wheat meat call for eggs to be used as a binder. If you are on an egg-restricted diet, the whites, alone, may be used with no appreciable difference.

Making Raw Wheat Meat

USING ELECTRIC MIXER WITH DOUGH HOOK

10 Cups flour*
5 Cups cold water

* Use whole wheat for "beef" and other red meats; white flour for "chicken, shrimp" etc. and other white or light meats.

MIXING:

Combine the flour and water in the mixing bowl. Using the dough hook, knead for 5 minutes. (The proportion of flour to water need not be precise. What is needed is enough to make the consistency of bread dough.) Cover the bowl with plastic wrap or a towel to prevent drying out and let it rest in the refrigerator or a cool place a minimum of 20 minutes while the gluten further develops. If desired, it may be covered with water and placed in the refrigerator overnight.

WASHING:

After the dough has rested, divide into 1/4ths and work with one portion at a time, keeping the remainder covered while you work. Place a piece of dough in a large colander which is, in turn, placed in a larger bowl of cold water. While keeping it immersed in the water at all times, stretch and compress the dough, trying to keep it intact while the bran and starch are washed out.

In a matter of minutes the mass will resemble bubble gum in texture and a few bran flakes may still be present. Do not try to wash them all out, a few are normal.

The water remaining from the washing should never be thrown away as it has many other uses we will discuss later. Pour it into a gallon jar or other such container for further use.

The "rubbery glob" you now have should be washed briefly in a bowl of fresh cold water and then placed in another bowl, covered with water to wait while your prepare the rest. The material you have created is raw wheat meat, or gluten, which, by employing various methods of preparation, becomes ground beef, roasts, chicken chunks or roasts or nuggets, shrimp, clam, etc.

USING HAND KNEADED METHOD

7 Cups flour* **3 Cups cold water**

* Use whole wheat for "beef" and other red meats; white flour for "chicken, shrimp" etc. and other white or light meats.

Mix together in a large mixing bowl, adding more water, if needed, to achieve a bread dough consistency. It will not require kneading if it is covered with plastic or a cloth and allowed to rest for at least 30 minutes to allow the gluten to develop. If desired, cover with water and place in the refrigerator overnight.

Follow the directions for the electric mixer method, above, for the washing procedure.

USING THE WATER:

The milky water remaining from the washing of the wheat meat contains most of the vitamins and minerals found in the wheat. It is too valuable to throw away. If allowed to sit, undisturbed for at least an hour, it will separate into three distinct layers, each with different properties and uses. For greatest ease in separating, place in the refrigerator overnight.

The top clear layer of **WATER**, when poured off can be used to water the house plants, livestock or pets, used in mixing powdered milk or in fruit drinks, making bread . . . anywhere clear water would be used.

The second layer of **STARCH** is valuable as a thickener in gravies, puddings, soups, stews and sauces. Use it in breads, homemade ice cream, even floor wax and hand lotions.

To use as a thickener, use anywhere from 4 to 7 Tablespoons of thick raw starch to every 2 Cups of liquid in your recipe. The results are quite like cornstarch. Cooked wheat starch is an essential ingredient in some of the breakfast cereal recipes, **(See Breakfast section).**

This starch has a very short "shelf-life". It should be kept refrigerated and stored no longer than 2 days. For longer storage, keep in the freezer.

The third layer consists of **BRAN**. With the emphasis on the importance of bran in today's diet, this sediment which remains on the bottom of the vessel can hardly be thought of as a by-product! Once disdained as lowly animal feed, a bran product now occupies almost every shelf in the supermarket. Keep it to use in crackers and breads, using **1/2** cup bran to every 2 cups of flour. It is also good in cakes, cookies and pie crusts.

(A recipe for bran flakes may be found in the breakfast section)

Bran, rinsed until the water runs clear, will keep 4-6 days in the refrigerator. If kept longer, it should be frozen or powdered. To prepare powdered bran, bake in a 300° oven 20-25 minutes on a greased cookie sheet. Let cool and grind in a blender. Store on cupboard shelf and use as needed.

FLAVORING AND COOKING

BEEF

GROUND BEEF is probably the most universally and conveniently used form of beef, so we will begin with it. There are two approaches to using ground beef; As an addition to casseroles, as fillings, anywhere you would normally add fried, crumbled ground beef . . . and in recipes where raw hamburger would be shaped and formed such as in meatballs, meat loaf, chopped sirloin steaks, etc.

We will show you how to make cooked, crumbled "ground beef" here, and recipes at the end of this chapter will guide you on the other methods for each recipe.

Take the raw, washed gluten previously made and form it into balls the size of an orange. Place on greased cookie sheets and bake in a 350° oven for 45 minutes until firm and leathery. (The tough leathery texture helps to give the meaty texture when it is ground.)

Remove from oven and let cool. Tear into pieces and put through a food or meat grinder. When ground, it has the appearance of ground beef. A food processor may be used, but the texture will not be quite the same.

Ingredients

2 1/2 Cups moderately packed ground gluten
2 Tablespoons beef soup base (amount may vary among brands)
2 Tablespoons vegetable oil
1/4 teaspoon garlic powder
1/4 Cup finely minced onion, OR
2 1/2 Tablespoons dehydrated onion flakes flakes
2 Tablespoons white flour
2 large eggs

Mix all the ingredients together in a large bowl and press onto a greased cookie sheet. Bake in 300° oven 15-20 minutes, or until the eggs are set. Cool and tear into small bits to resemble cooked hamburger. Add to soups, stews, casseroles, etc. just before serving. If allowed to cook in a dish as would regular ground beef, too much liquid is absorbed and the texture is lost.

ROAST BEEF is made by one of three methods. It needs to be sliced paper thin and served with a sauce. When cut in strips it can be added in casseroles or Stroganoff, just before serving. Cubes can be cut and heated in barbecue sauce; make sure they are cut no larger than a pair of dice for the best results.

1. Cloth sack method:

Construct sacks, or tubes of clean muslin, 2½″ in diameter and 5 inches in length. Pack full of washed, raw gluten and tie the ends securely. Place in a vessel and cover with a broth made of 4 Tablespoons beef soup base to each 2 quarts of water. For the long, slow simmering time involved, a crockpot is most economical, but it can be simmered on the stovetop or in the oven at 350°. Cook, covered, 6-8 hours, or overnight.

When sufficiently cooked, it will have the chewy texture of beef. To achieve a chewier texture, it may be placed on a greased cookie sheet and dried somewhat in a 300° oven for about 30 minutes.

2. Foil method:

Form the washed, raw gluten into 2½″ x 5″ cylinders. Roll tightly in foil. Simmer in water to cover for 2 hours. Unwrap and drop into boiling broth made from 4 Tablespoons beef soup base to 2 quarts of water. Simmer 6-8 hours, or overnight.

3. Greased tin method:

Fill a well-greased 1 pound coffee can, (or similar can), 1/2 full with raw washed gluten. Make a broth of 4 Tablespoons beef soup base to 2 quarts of water and cover the gluten to a depth of 2″. Lift the ball of gluten to assure the broth reaches all sides. Place in a 350° oven for 3-4 hours until broth is nearly all gone. Remove from the tin.

BEEF STEAK is made by rolling and stretching the gluten as thin as you can. It is very springy and bouncy, but persistence pays, in this case.

With a sharp knife, cut into steak shaped pieces and drop into a pot of boiling broth made from 4 Tablespoons beef soup base in 2 quarts of water. Simmer 2-3 hours until the texture resembles that of beef.

If desired, the texture may be improved by patting the steaks dry with paper toweling and drying in a 300° oven a few minutes. They should resemble thin beef "minute steaks".

CHICKEN

ROAST CHICKEN is made by one of three methods. It needs to be sliced paper thin and served with gravy. When cut into strips or diced into small cubes it can be added to casseroles, stir fried foods, or other dishes where cooked cubed chicken would normally be added. When ground, roast chicken becomes the main ingredient in a delicious chicken salad, served plain or as a sandwich filling.

1. Cloth sack method:

Construct sacks, or tubes of clean muslin, 2½" in diameter and 5" in length. Pack full of washed, raw gluten and tie the ends securely. Place in a vessel and cover with a broth made of 4 Tablespoons chicken soup base to each 2 quarts of water. For the long, slow simmering time involved, a crockpot is most economical, but it can be simmered on the stovetop or in the oven at 350°. Cook, covered, 6-8 hours, or overnight. When sufficiently cooked, it will have the chewy texture of chicken. To achieve a chewier texture, it may be placed on a greased cookie sheet and dried somewhat in a 300° oven for about 30 minutes.

2. Foil method:

Form the washed, raw gluten into 2½" by 5" cylinders. Roll tightly in foil. Simmer in water to cover for 2 hours. Unwrap and drop into boiling broth made from 4 Tablespoons chicken soup base to 2 quarts of water. Simmer 6-8 hours, or overnight.

3. Greased tin method:

Fill a well-greased 1 pound coffee can, (or similar can), 1/2 full with raw washed gluten. Make a broth of 4 Tablespoons chicken soup base to 2 quarts of water and cover the gluten to a depth of 2 inches. Lift the ball of gluten to assure the broth reaches all sides. Place in a 350° oven for 3-4 hours until broth is nearly all gone. Remove from the tin.

CHICKEN CHUNKS are a tasty addition to Chinese dishes, salads, and stews. Prepare a broth of 4 Tablespoons chicken soup base to 2 quarts of boiling water and drop into it pieces of raw gluten which you have pinched off with your fingers. If desired, kitchen shears may be used to snip pieces directly into the broth. Simmer 1-2 hours, depending upon the size. To use, add just before serving in hot dishes, or use, chilled in cold dishes.

CHICKEN NUGGETS are everyone's favorite. These have no saturated fat, to speak of. Roll the washed raw gluten to a thickness of 1/2". Sprinkle the surface lightly with chicken soup base. Roll up tightly and wrap in foil or fabric. (tie securely at both ends). Keep the rolls to a diameter of 1½". If using foil, simmer in water till set, about 1½ hours. Then simmer in broth, 4 Tablespoons chicken soup base to 2 quarts of water, for 4-6 hours. If using fabric, eliminate the water-simmering and simmer in the above broth 6-8 hours. Cut in 1/2"-3/4" slices. Dip in milk, roll in flour, dip in beaten egg, then roll in fine cracker or bread crumbs. Fry in hot oil until golden crispy. Serve with your favorite sauce. See Sauce section in the "Bind It Together or Dress It Up" chapter.

PORK

PORK ROASTS, STEAKS AND ETC. are made in the same manner as the chicken with the exception of the soup base. To simulate a pork flavor, mix half chicken with half beef soup base, or obtain pork flavored soup base.

Shrimp And FishStrips

SHRIMP AND FISH STRIPS have become, to many, a fond memory. Now, with this easy recipe you will find it possible not only to serve a crunchy tray of appetizers at a party, but a genuine "fill-em-up" meal for your shrimp lovers.

There are two methods to achieve the shrimp or fish flavor. One entails the saving of juice, or liquid from a previously used can of tuna. (Here the economy lies in the ability to provide two meals from the one can of tuna, or any other canned fish.) The other method utilizes the ever-versatile soup base, a clam flavor in this case. Be sure not to use fish bouillon as the results would be very unsatisfactory.

Method #1 - Tuna liquid:

Make 1/2 recipe raw, washed gluten. Cut pieces very small and flatten, shaping into approximate shrimp shapes. In a medium sized oven-proof pan, put 2 Cups of water and 1 Tablespoon each salt and oil. Into this drop the shrimp pieces and boil 45 minutes. Remove from heat and place the pan with the shrimp into a 300° to 350° oven for 2-3 hours. (Test for proper texture before continuing.) Remove with a slotted spoon and press firmly between paper toweling to remove excess liquid. Place shrimp in a small bowl and cover it with the reserved liquid from a can of tuna or other canned fish. Turn the pieces over with the fingers until they all have been coated. Cover and refrigerate for 2-3 hours. Remove and once again, press out all the liquid. Dip the pieces briefly in milk, then in flour. Dip them again in beaten egg and roll in seasoned bread or cracker crumbs. Fry in hot oil until golden brown and crispy. Serve with cocktail sauce. **(see Index)**

Method #2- soup base:

Follow above; however, add 1 1/2 Tablespoons clam soup base to the water. Omit the marinating in tuna liquid.

FISH STRIPS are made in essentially the same manner as the shrimp. However, instead of cutting the shrimp pieces, the washed raw gluten is rolled out on a moistened surface to 1/2″ thickness. This is then cut into 1″ x 1/2″

strips. The directions are the same for the strips and they are served with tartar sauce. See Index for recipe.

NOTE: To achieve an even chewier texture, the gluten may be placed in the refrigerator, covered with water for two days before starting with any of the shrimp steps. When ready to begin, drain and proceed as above.

Now that you have the basics of preparing the elementary "meats", there is no end to the number and variety of dishes you can create. The following are a few recipes we enjoy that you might try. Then, armed with your new knowledge and skills, you can set out to adapt any of your own particular favorites.

Wheat Meat Wieners

Forget about the world needing a better mousetrap. What it needs is a hot dog you are not afraid to eat. So here it is: a hot dog that is actually good for you.

This recipe uses a special spice for the seasoning to achieve the hot dog flavor. It is Bologna-flavored **Spice'n Slice**™, made by Grandma LaMure's **Spice'n Slice**™. Although I have found it in our local Farmer's Cooperative food section, it is not readily available. It may be ordered from Seagull Family Products, Inc., P. O. Box 26051, Phoenix, Arizona 84068. The telephone number is (602) 861-4094.

To make the wieners, use the recipe for light meat, using white flour. Roll the washed gluten, or raw wheat meat, into shapes approximating store-bought wieners. Wrap tightly in foil and boil 2½ to 3 hours in water until firm. With the **Spice'n Slice**™ make a broth, using 1 Tablespoon from each packet combined in 3 Cups of water. Unwrap the "wieners" and drop them into the broth which has been brought to a boil. Simmer for about 20 minutes until the desired flavor is reached.

Serve in homemade hot dog buns with homemade catsup, mayonnaise and mustard. The recipes are found in the index.

Meatballs

These are prepared in a manner similar to the wheat meat ground beef.

2½ Cups moderately packed ground gluten **2 eggs**
2 Tablespoons beef soup base (more/less depending upon saltiness)
2 Tablespoons white flour **1/4 teaspoon garlic powder**
1/4 Cup chopped onion (leave some larger for texture)

Mix all the ingredients together in a medium sized bowl. Using the fingers of one hand against the palm of the other, form meatballs a little smaller than a walnut. The mixture should be quite moist. add another egg if it is too dry.

Place on a paper plate, no more than 5 at a time, and cover with plastic film. Microwave on high just until egg is set. Time will vary with individual ovens.

For conventional ovens, add 2 Tablespoons of vegetable oil to the mixture and form as above. Bake in a 300° oven just until the eggs are set.

These freeze beautifully for use later, or can be used in a recipe right away.

For SPAGHETTI AND MEATBALLS, heat homemade spaghetti sauce, **(See index)** and cook pasta (See index). Add the meatballs to the hot sauce and heat through. Do not over cook. Serve on top of hot, cooked pasta. Garnish with sprinkled Parmesan cheese, if desired.

Salisbury Steak or Hamburger Patties

These are made in the same manner as the wheat meatballs in the above recipe. Instead of rolling into small balls, a portion is patted into a patty shape and either cooked in the oven until set, or fried in a lightly greased pan. They are served with a ladle of Salisbury gravy poured over the top.

Beef or Salisbury Gravy*

2 Tablespoons butter or margarine
1/2 Onion, thinly sliced
1 Tablespoon flour or cornstarch
1 1/2 Tablespoons beef soup base
1/2 teaspoon Kitchen Bouquet™
1 teaspoon Worcestershire Sauce
1 1/4 Cups water
1 teaspoon onion powder
1/2 teaspoon garlic powder

* Add 1/4 Cup chopped mushrooms for Salisbury Gravy

In a small saucepan, sauté the mushrooms and onions in the butter. Blend the flour or cornstarch with the water until no lumps remain and stir it into the mushroom mixture. Add 1 Tablespoon of the beef soup base and the remaining ingredients. Stir until smooth and slightly thickened. Taste and, if not too salty, stir in remaining **1/2** Tablespoon soup base to suit your taste.

Sloppy Joes, Wheat Meat Style

2 Cups wheat meat Ground Beef
1/4 teaspoon pepper
1 Tablespoon brown sugar
3/4 Cup onion, chopped
1 Tablespoon vinegar
Salt, to taste
1 1/2 Cups homemade tomato sauce or catsup (See index)
1 Tablespoon prepared mustard (See index)
6 Homemade hamburger buns (See Index)

In a large skillet, heat together all the ingredients except the wheat meat ground beef. Simmer, uncovered, for one minute. Stir in the wheat meat and serve immediately over the hamburger buns which have been split and toasted. Serves 6.

Sausage-Flavored Wheat Meat Zucchini Halves

5 Medium zucchini
1/4 teaspoon dried thyme
1/2 Cup Parmesan cheese, grated
2 Tablespoons vegetable oil
1/2 Cup Mozzarella cheese, shredded
1/4 Cup onion, chopped
3/4 Cup water
1/2 teaspoon garlic powder
Paprika for garnish
crushed pepper to taste
$1^{1}/_{2}$ Cups uncooked ground wheat meat*
1/2 Cup finely crushed crackers or bread crumbs
1/4 teaspoon beef soup base, or salt to taste

* flavored to taste with Sausage seasoning. **See index**.

(This recipe uses raw wheat meat, so prepare as you would for meatballs, omitting the cooking stage.)

Cut the zucchini in half, lengthwise. Scoop out the pulp, leaving 1/4 inch shells, reserving 1 Cup of the pulp. Place the zucchini shells, cut side down, in a large skillet. Add the water, cover and simmer for 3 minutes or until tender. Remove from skillet, drain and sprinkle with a little salt. Chop the reserved pulp and add to the raw wheat ground beef in a large bowl. Mix in the remaining ingredients, excluding the paprika. Spoon equally into the zucchini shells and sprinkle with paprika. Bake, covered, in a 350 ° oven for 10 to 15 minutes, or until the eggs are set. Serves 5.

Stuffed Chicken Rolls

For this recipe you will need approximately two wheat meat chicken roasts, 5″ x $2^{1}/_{2}$″. Where ordinarily we recommend slicing paper thin, in this case they need to be sliced thick enough to hold their shape when rolled.

8 Lengthwise slices of chicken roast
1 Tablespoon butter or margarine
3/4 Cup medium onion, finely chopped
1/4 Cup raisins or chopped dried apricots
3/4 Cup cooked rice
2 Tablespoons dried parsley, or fresh, minced
1 teaspoon homemade curry powder (See index)
1 teaspoon brown sugar
1/8 teaspoon garlic powder
1/2 teaspoon poultry seasoning
$1^{1}/_{2}$ Tablespoons vegetable oil

Melt butter or margarine in a skillet and add the onions. Sauté until soft and translucent, stirring frequently. Add the rice, raisins or apricots, parsley, curry powder, brown sugar, poultry seasoning, and garlic powder. Mix well and divide into 8 portions. Spoon one portion on each slice of roast and roll up, securing with a toothpick. Serve with chicken gravy (See next page) Serves 4.

Oriental-Style Wheat Meatball Salad

30 Wheat meatballs (See index)
1 8-Ounce can pineapple chunks
2 Medium green peppers, cut into 1/2″ squares
3 Medium stalks celery, sliced diagonally
1/2 Cup + 1 Tablespoon packed brown sugar
2 Tablespoons soy sauce
3 Medium carrots, sliced
1/2 Cup dry white wine
1/3 Cup homemade vinegar
2 Tablespoons cornstarch

Drain the pineapple and reserve juice. Add water to the reserved juice to make 3/4 Cup liquid. In a large bowl, mix the pineapple chunks, carrots, celery, green pepper and meatballs. Set aside. In a small sauce pan, mix the brown sugar, cornstarch, pineapple liquid, vinegar, wine and soy sauce. Cook and stir until the mixture thickens. Pour, while hot, over the wheat meat balls and the other ingredients. Cover and chill before serving. Garnish with shredded lettuce and tomatoes. Serves 4 to 5.

"Chicken" or "Turkey" and Dressing

This is prepared by slicing the wheat meat chicken roast paper thin. Place a scoop or large spoonful of basic stuffing mix, (See index) on a greased baking sheet. Lay a slice of the roast on top and cover with gravy. Repeat until you have a sufficient number assembled. Heat in a 350° oven just until warmed through, taking great care not to over cook. When served with the usual holiday fixings, most people cannot tell the difference from the "real thing".

Chicken Gravy

1 Tablespoon butter or margarine
1 Tablespoon flour or cornstarch
1½ Tablespoons chicken soup base
1 teaspoon parsley flakes
1/2 teaspoon garlic powder
1 Pinch fresh ground pepper
1½ teaspoons onion powder
1/4 teaspoon poultry seasoning, if desired
1¼ Cups water, milk, soy milk or Milk♥Lite®

Mix 1 Tablespoon of the chicken soup base with the remaining ingredients and stir until smooth. Heat and stir over medium heat until slightly thickened. Taste and add the remaining 1/2 Tablespoon soup base, a little at a time, until the desired flavor is reached. As soup bases vary in their saltiness, let your own taste be your guide.

Corn

There are many types of corn grown and loved by nearly everyone. We are all familiar with the ear of hot sweet corn, dripping with butter. For our purposes here, however, we will restrict ourselves to the discussion of the corn found in our food storage: Dent Corn, commonly known as Field Corn. This is a very hard corn with a characteristic dent in the top of the kernel when dried. And dried is the way we find it, for it is never eaten fresh. Used primarily for livestock feed, we recommend it for it is inexpensive, readily available, and grinds into fine cornmeal. It also makes good hominy and masa, which will be discussed later. The only caution would be to buy **FEED** corn, not **SEED** corn which likely would have been treated with a fungicide which would render it toxic.

It is best, when grinding corn, not to use a stone grinder. Grinding corn can glaze and render the stone worthless. However, if this is unavoidable, be sure to grind coarsely and then run some wheat through afterward.

Home-ground cornmeal still contains the germ of the grain, as contrasted to the commercial product. This results in a shorter shelf-life, so grind a small amount at a time and keep it in the refrigerator to prevent it from going rancid.

Tamale Pie

FILLING:

1½ pounds ground beef or 3 Cups wheat meat hamburger
1 large onion, chopped — **1 teaspoon oregano**
2 Tablespoons chili powder — **1/4 teaspoon garlic powder**
3 Cups cooked pinto or pink beans — **1 teaspoon salt**
2 Cups tomato sauce — **2 Cups water**
1 roasted, peeled green chili, chopped (or use canned)
1½ Cups shredded homemade Colby cheese

TOPPING:

1¼ Cups cornmeal — **1/4 Cup flour**
1/2 Cup powdered milk or Milk♥Lite® — **1/2 teaspoon salt**
1/4 Cup vegetable shortening — **1 egg**
3/4 teaspoon baking powder — **1½ Cups water**

Grease an oven-proof baking dish. In a large skillet, brown the ground beef with the salt and garlic powder. **(If using wheat meat hamburger, omit**

the salt and garlic powder and this step.) For the filling combine all the ingredients except cheese with the ground beef, **(or here is where you add the wheat meat, if using.)**. Pour into the greased dish and place in a 350° oven while you prepare the topping.

To prepare the topping, stir together the dry ingredients. Add water, egg, and shortening and beat until smooth. Remove the dish from the oven and sprinkle with 1 Cup of the cheese. Spoon the topping around the margin of the hot filling and sprinkle it with the remaining cheese. Bake at 400° for 15 to 20 minutes. Serves 8.

Southern Corn Bread

The secret to the success of this recipe is to use a heavy, preferably cast iron, skillet and have it sizzling hot when the batter is poured in. Unlike most other cornbread recipes, this one bakes on top of the stove.

1 Cup flour
1 Cup milk, soy milk or Milk♥Lite®
2 teaspoons baking powder
scant 1/2 teaspoon salt
1 teaspoon sugar
1 egg, beaten
1 Cup cornmeal
1/4 Cup shortening

Mix the dry ingredients together in a large bowl. Place a small heavy skillet over high heat and add the shortening. While the shortening melts and the skillet heats, add the egg and milk to the dry ingredients. Lifting the hot skillet carefully, pour the hot oil into the batter. Mix it thoroughly and immediately pour the batter into the hot, oil-coated skillet. Cover with a lid, turn the heat to the lowest possible setting, and cook until set. When set, carefully turn the cornbread over, using two pancake turners. Continue to cook until golden brown on the bottom. Serve immediately. Makes approximately 9 servings.

Hominy

The procedure for making hominy is much the same as for masa. Both are radically different from grinding as for cornmeal, but not at all difficult. The hulls need to be removed and this is accomplished in many fashions. A Bite Of Independence goes into greater detail than we have room for here. We will restrict ourselves to the use of hot builder's lime, found at lumberyards or 'do-it-yourself' supply outlets. It is cheap and lasts nearly forever, if kept dry.

8 Cups dried corn
3/4 Cup hot builder's lime
Water

Put corn in a large, non-aluminum pot and cover with at least 2 inches of water. Stir in the lime and bring to a boil. Boil for 45 minutes, stirring frequently to keep from sticking. Add additional water if necessary to keep the water level constant. By this time, the skins should slip when a kernel is pressed between the fingers. Place in a colander and rinse well under a forceful stream of water to remove the lime and the hulls. Rinse 4 to 5 times, rubbing the kernels together and against the mesh of the colander or sieve. Rinse the pot well and return the corn to it, where, covered again with fresh water, it will cook 2 to 3 hours until the hominy is tender. Use in recipes, or enjoy hot with salt and butter.

MASA

Masa is the basis of the corn tortilla, the staple bread of Mexico. Tortillas are also the basic ingredient in many Mexican dishes, enchiladas being but one of many. With your stored corn, you are never far away from a meal. Masa is very perishable when fresh, so use it right away, or keep no longer than 3 days in the refrigerator. Fortunately, it freezes well.

Making Masa

2 Quarts dried corn
3/4 Cup hot builder's lime

Cover corn with at least three inches of water in a non-aluminum pot. Stir in the lime, cover and boil at least 45 minutes, stirring frequently to prevent sticking. Add water, if needed, to maintain the level. The water should, by this time, be thick, with the skins slipping easily from the kernels. To test for doneness, pinch a kernel in half. You should see a white streak running down the center. Rinse the corn in a colander under a forceful stream of water, rubbing the kernels together to remove the hulls. When thoroughly rinsed, run through a grinder. Be sure to use a wet-corn grinder, or the fine-grind blade on the meat grinder. A little water can be added during the grinding, should the consistency prove too thick.

The masa is now ready to use as is, or freeze for later use.

Corn Tortillas

Add enough water to the prepared masa to make a manageable dough. For authentic Mexican flavor, add no salt. Form into balls the size of walnuts and place between two sheets of waxed paper or damp cloth. Roll with a rolling pin until very thin and about 6 inches across. Or you can place between two sheets of waxed paper and press in a tortilla press. Bake on an ungreased griddle until both sides are lightly flecked with brown spots. They should still be soft. If the tortillas stick, lightly wipe the griddle with an oiled paper towel.

Use right away or store in a tightly closed plastic bag. You'll find that they freeze well.

To resoften for later use, heat on an ungreased griddle, or in a little fat.

Enchiladas with Beef or Wheat Meat

2 dozen corn tortillas **2 medium onions, chopped**
1 pound ground beef , <u>**OR**</u>
2 Cups wheat meat hamburger or wheat beef roast
4 Cups of red enchilada sauce (see Index)
1 pound shredded homemade Colby or Monterey Jack cheese,
Sour cream for topping (optional)

To make the filling with beef: Brown the ground beef in a medium skillet. Stir in one of the chopped onions and sauté until wilted. Moisten with 1/2 to 3/4 Cup of the enchilada sauce.

If using wheat meat: Sauté the onion in a little oil in a the skillet. Crumble the wheat meat burger or slice the roast as thinly as possible and mix it with the wilted onions and 1/2 to 3/4 Cup of the sauce.

To assemble: Soften the tortilla in hot oil in a skillet. Put a big spoonful of the filling in the center of the tortilla, sprinkle with some of the cheese and remaining onion and roll up. Place a layer of the sauce in the bottom of a baking pan and lay the enchiladas in it, seam side down. When they are all rolled, pour more sauce over the top and sprinkle with additional cheese. Bake at 350° until bubbly. Serve with a topping of sour cream and additional sauce, if desired. Makes 2 dozen.

Soybeans... A Dairy In A Bean

Coming from China some 3,000 years ago, this protein-rich legume serves both as a dairy and a meat substitute. Containing more than twice the protein of beef or fish, three times more than eggs, and eleven times that of milk, is it any wonder that the soybean is known as "meat without bones", or the "cow of the East"?

Dry soybeans store well and are an invaluable component of a food storage program. When properly prepared, they can nutritionally and tastily fulfill a family's dairy requirements and treats, plus provide protein in the form of meat extenders or even replacements.

SOY MILK may be used whenever one would ordinarily use dairy milk. When used in cooking, it can hardly be discerned from cow's milk. Sweetened to taste with a little sugar, it makes a very acceptable beverage. Known for its easy digestibility, and containing no cholesterol, it forms the base for nutritious baby formulas, not to mention a healthful, complete protein drink for sensitive stomachs.

Making Soy Milk

This is not a difficult procedure. The beans need to be soaked first; either overnight, or cover with boiling water and let stand four hours. One pound of beans (about 2 1/4 Cups) is a convenient amount to work with and should yield about one gallon of soy milk.

Rinse well and place one cup of soaked beans in a blender. Add two cups of water and blend until smooth. Pour the contents into a double thickness of cheesecloth, or similar porous material, and wring and squeeze the milk into a container. Add another cup of water to the mass and re-squeeze to obtain the remaining milk. Repeat the procedure with the remaining beans and measure the resulting milk. There should be one gallon; if not, add more water to equal that measure.

Soy needs to be cooked to be digestible to humans, so pour it into a saucepan and bring to a boil over medium heat. Reduce heat and simmer for 20 minutes, stirring to prevent scorching. Add sugar and salt to taste and refrigerate as you would cow's milk.

This recipe makes a regular strength milk. For a richer milk, suitable for **WHIPPING**, or for any use where **CREAM** would be appropriate, blend in the blender at the rate of 1 Cup beans to 1 Cup of water for a yield of 1/2 gallon.

Making Tofu

Tofu is a wonderful food. Not just a buzzword of the "yuppie generation", it is truly a marvel that makes foods, once thought sinfully rich, actually good for you. It can take its place anywhere on the table during any course and blend right in. No one knows it is there. From the first course salad where it appears as the "Thousand Island" dressing, to the gooey, decadent "cheese-cake" for dessert, tofu is right at home.

This recipe can be doubled or even tripled with consistent results. When you become familiar with tofu's many uses, you will want to make large batches. One word of caution, however. Do not expect the same tofu characteristics once it is frozen. When frozen, tofu changes texture and actually assumes the qualities of meat. It makes a terrific **TUNA EXTENDER** in tuna salad, etc. Having no apparent flavor of its own, it picks up that of the tuna and nearly doubles the amount! Simply place the frozen tofu in a bowl and pour boiling water over it. Shred pieces from the margins with a fork as it thaws. When mixed with the tuna, salad dressing, onions, celery, etc., one is hard pressed to tell the difference.

Tofu

3 1/2 Cups very hot water **1/4 Cup cool water**
1 3/4 Cups presoaked and rinsed soybeans (See Soy Milk)
1 Tablespoon Epsom Salts, or Sea Salt, or Gypsum

Put the beans in a blender with just enough of the hot water to blend to a thick gruel. Pour into a dampened cheesecloth and wring and knead to extract the milk. Mix more of the reserved hot water in the mash and knead again. Repeat with all the water to obtain the maximum amount of milk from the beans. **(See *Note below)**

To make the soy digestible to humans, pour into a saucepan and bring to a boil. Reduce heat and simmer for 20 minutes, stirring to prevent scorching. Meanwhile, dissolve the Epsom salt, or whichever coagulant you've chosen in the 1/4 Cup water. Turn off the heat, leaving the pan on the burner. Give one final, circular stir of the milk and pour the dissolved salt into the center. Cover with a lid and leave undisturbed for 10 to 20 minutes while coagulation takes place. Do not jar, or otherwise disturb the forming curds. Meanwhile, line a colander or tofu press with dampened cheesecloth. When the time has elapsed, gently lift the curds from the pot with a slotted spoon and place in the cheesecloth. Cover with the folded over cheesecloth and apply pressure. If using a colander, place a plate on the top and upon that, set a weight. If convenient, placing the whole unit in a sink of cold water while the pressing takes place helps to speed up the cooling process. If not, place in the refrigerator. When the tofu has thoroughly cooled, approximately 15 minutes (depending upon the size of the batch), it is ready to use.

Tofu can keep for several days in the refrigerator, covered with water or in a tightly sealed bag. Every day it grows a little stronger in flavor, so its uses are dictated by its age. Use the freshest made for mild flavored foods, and the older for things with more "body".

***NOTE:** The pulp remaining is called **OKARA** and is too valuable to throw away. A few spoonfuls in a bread dough helps the loaf to hold together when sliced, and it also has the property of helping the loaf to slip easily from the pan when baked. It is useful as an extender in ground beef recipes such as meat loafs and casseroles, and even as an egg substitute in many recipes. Simply replace one egg with one teaspoon of okara.

The time will come when you will wonder how you ever managed before tofu. With the few pennies it takes to make, compared to the amount you spend at the supermarket for a teeny little block, you can afford to experiment. Soon you will be singing the praises of the lowly soybean, too!

Soy Peanut Butter Extender

Blend soaked soybeans with enough water in a blender to make a gruel. Cook over moderate-low heat 20 minutes, stirring to prevent scorching. Allow to cool sufficiently to handle, then squeeze through cheesecloth to extract the milk.

The cooked **OKARA** remaining is the material used in this procedure. The okara needs to be blended smooth in the blender, then mixed with the peanut butter - two parts peanut butter to one part okara. Allow it to meld several hours in the refrigerator before use, and stir before using. Make no more than can be used within a week.

Soy Flour

Cover pre-soaked soy beans with water and bring to a boil in a large saucepan. Lower heat to simmer and cook for 20 minutes. Drain well.

Grind the beans in a blender, or food processor on the coarsest setting.

Spread the resulting grits on a baking sheet and bake in a 150° oven for one hour. Grind in a grain mill. (Do not use a stone grinder.)

Soy Nuts

(See recipe in Snacks section)

Tofu-Extended Scrambled Eggs

To extend the amount of scrambled eggs, simply replace one egg with 1/4 Cup of fresh, crumbled tofu. Scramble as usual.

Tofu Crepes

3/4 Cup unbleached flour
1/2 teaspoon vanilla
1/3 Cup water
2/3 Cup milk, Soy milk or Milk♥Lite®
3 Tablespoons tofu
1 egg
1½ teaspoons baking powder

Place all the ingredients in a blender and whirl until smooth. Allow to rest for 20 minutes. Spray the bottom of a small skillet with nonstick spray and heat over medium to low heat. Pour a small amount of batter into the pan and tip it to coat evenly. Cook until set and the top is dry. Flip out onto a wire rack to cool and repeat. Stack between squares of waxed paper. These are good with sweetened cottage cheese and fruit, cream cheese, or any of your favorite crepes fillings.

Tofu-Extended Cottage Cheese

Mash tofu into cottage cheese-sized particles and salt to taste. Mix with an equal amount of cottage cheese and add cream or fruit to taste. Store in the refrigerator.

Soy Yogurt

2 Cups rich homemade soy milk
1/4 **Cup fresh cultured yogurt** (be sure it contains active culture) **OR**
1/4 **Cup commercial starter culture** (Use Lactobacillus acidophilus, or Lactobacillus bulgarius. Available at most health food stores)

Heat soy milk just to boiling point. Remove from heat and cool to 100° to 110°. Mix with the yogurt or with commercial starter which has been reconstituted per package instructions. Place in an incubator at approximately 110° for 4 to 5 hours. **(See the Cheese and Yogurt Section.)**

Soy Milk Gravy

1/4 Cup unbleached flour
2 Cups soy milk
Pepper (optional)
4 Tablespoons oil or butter
Chicken or beef soup base, to taste

In a medium sized skillet over medium heat, stir the flour until it browns. Stir in the oil or butter until thoroughly blended. Gradually add the soy milk, stirring constantly until it thickens. Season to taste with the soup base and pepper.

Soy White Sauce

Substitute soy milk in any white sauce or milk sauce recipe.

Tofu Sour Cream

1½ Cups mashed tofu
3 Tablespoons cream cheese
1/4 Cup dairy sour cream OR
1 Tablespoon sour cream flavoring mix

Place all the ingredients in a blender and blend until smooth. Chill.

Thousand Island Salad Dressing

1/4 pound soft fresh tofu, mashed
1/2 Cup homemade catsup
4 Tablespoons sweet pickle relish
1/2 teaspoon onion powder
1/8 teaspoon garlic powder
1/4 teaspoon salt
3 Tablespoons green olives, minced (optional)

Place all the ingredients but the relish and olives in a blender and whirl until smooth. Stir in the relish and olives, if desired. Chill.

Bleu Cheese Salad Dressing

3 Tablespoons cream cheese
1 Tablespoon grated Parmesan cheese
1/4 teaspoon garlic powder
1/2 Cup tofu
4 teaspoons Bleu Cheese flavor Snack'n Dip™ †

† (Flavoring by Watkins Inc., Winona, MI 55987)

Blend tofu, Bleu Cheese flavoring, Parmesan and garlic powder until smooth. Stir in cream cheese, but leave in small lumps for texture. Keep refrigerated.

No-Egg Foo Yung

1½ Tablespoons vegetable oil
1 Cup mushrooms, sliced
1/4 Cup pimientos, minced
2¼ teaspoons baking powder
1/2 Cup green onions, sliced
2 Cups bean sprouts (See index)
1 Cup shredded cabbage
2 pounds tofu
2½ Tablespoons soy sauce
1 Cup flour
1 Cup sliced water chestnuts
3/4 Cup snow peas

Sauté mushrooms, pimientos, snow peas, onions, water chestnuts and cabbage in oil in a large skillet. When tender, add bean sprouts. Remove from heat and set aside.

In a bowl, combinetofu and soy sauce, beating until smooth and creamy. Thoroughly mix in flour and baking powder. Combine with the vegetables and spoon onto an oiled baking sheet, making 10 to 12 five inch rounds, about 1/2"thick. Bake in a 325° oven for 30 minutes, turn over and continue baking 15 more minutes. Serve over rice or homemade Chow Mein noodles (See index), topped with onion gravy. Serves 10. Recipe may be halved.

Onion Gravy

2 Cups cold water
1/4 Cup thinly sliced onions
4 Tablespoons soy sauce
2 Tablespoons cornstarch
1/2 teaspoon soup base, or more, to taste
1/4 teaspoon sugar

Stir together in a small saucepan and cook over low heat until thickened.

Tofu Stuffed Green Peppers

4 Cups homemade tomato sauce
1½ Cups cooked rice
1/2 Cup onion, chopped
2 Tablespoons olive oil
4 teaspoons sugar
1 Cup fresh, frozen or canned corn
6 large bell peppers
2 small bay leaves
1/4 teaspoon garlic powder
1½ teaspoons sweet basil
2 teaspoons Oregano
1 pound tofu in 1/2″ cubes
Few twists of freshly ground pepper

Cut the tops from the peppers and remove the seeds and membranes. Partially cook the peppers in boiling water just until they lose their crispness, about 5 minutes. Drain them and set aside.

In a medium saucepan mix together the tomato sauce, garlic powder, bay leaves, basil, oregano, pepper and sugar. Simmer while you prepare the filling. In a large skillet sauté the onions in the olive oil. Add the tofu cubes, and when slightly brown add the corn, rice, and 1½ Cups of the sauce. Spoon the filling into each pepper and stand upright in a baking dish. Pour the remaining sauce over and bake at 350° for about 30 minuets. Serves 6.

Tofu "Meat Balls"

(These are a good substitute in spaghetti, etc.)

1/2 Cup (or to taste) crackers, or bread crumbs, or unbleached flour
1 pound tofu
4 Tablespoons soy sauce
2 Tablespoons peanut butter
1/3 Cup finely chopped onion
1/4 Cup Parmesan cheese
Vegetable oil
1/2 teaspoon dry mustard
1/4 teaspoon oregano
1/4 teaspoon sweet basil
1/8 teaspoon black pepper
1/2 teaspoon garlic powder

Mix all the ingredients together and roll into 1″ to 1½″ balls. Dredge in flour and brown in hot oil in a large skillet. Serve with spaghetti sauce. **(See index)**

Tofu Cheesecake

$1^2/_3$ Cups mashed tofu
1 Cup sugar
1/2 teaspoon vanilla
4 teaspoons lemon juice
2 Tablespoons powdered eggs
1/2 Cup vegetable oil
6 Tablespoons or 1/3 Cup Cream cheese
2 Tablespoons Clear Jel™ †

Place all the ingredients in a blender and whirl until smooth. Pour into a prepared graham cracker crust and top with your favorite fruit topping. Chill before serving.

† **Clear Jel™** is available at restaurant supply houses, food distributors, and most health food stores.

Chocolate Mint Tofu Ice Cream

2 Cups soy milk, milk or Milk♥Lite®
2 pounds soft tofu
1/4 teaspoon salt
$1^1/_2$ teaspoons peppermint extract
1/2 Cup cocoa
1 Cup vegetable oil
2 Cups sugar

Blend in a blender until smooth and creamy. Pour into hand operated or electric ice cream freezer and freeze according to manufacturer's directions. Makes 10 Cups

Apricot Tofu Ice Cream

4 Cups chopped apricots
3 Cups soy milk, milk or Milk♥Lite®
1/2 Cup lemon juice
1/2 pounds tofu
$1^1/_4$ Cups sugar
4 Tablespoons vanilla
1/4 teaspoon salt
1 Cup sugar

Mix the fruit, 1/2 Cup lemon juice and 1 Cup sugar together and let stand for one hour in the refrigerator to draw the juice. Combine with the remaining ingredients and blend until smooth in a blender. Freeze in hand operated or electric freezer per manufacturer's directions.

Makes a little more than $2^1/_2$ quarts. This is also good with peaches or strawberries.

Rice

While rice eaten in the Asian countries is generally brown rice with only the outer hull removed, that which we are more likely to find here is the more refined, white variety. Although far superior to white which has had much of the nutritive value milled away, brown rice does not posses the keeping qualities necessary for long term storage. To avoid rancidity, brown rice needs to be kept either in a cool dry place, or in the freezer. Of the thousands of varieties of rice, we will be concerned here with only three, classified by the length of grain. Long Grain, which cooks up in distinct separate grains, is sometimes called Patna, Bluebonnet or Rexora. Medium Grain has a softer kernel and results in a stickier, though fluffy dish. It can be found under the name Calrose, Blue Rose, Japan Rose, Nato, Zenith or Magnolia. Short Grain rice, found as Colusa, California Pearl or Calora is quite sticky when cooked.

Cooking Rice Is Very Simple

Use 1 cup uncooked rice to 2 cups of liquid for regular milled white rice or use $2^1/_2$ cups water or other liquid to 1 cup of brown rice. Add 1 teaspoon of salt and bring to a boil in a 3 quart saucepan with a tight-fitting lid. Stir once or twice and lower heat to simmer. Keep tightly covered, (do not even peek), for 15 minutes when cooking white rice, and for 45 minutes when cooking brown rice. Test, and if necessary, replace the lid for an additional 3 to 5 minutes.

If you prefer a drier texture, fluff the rice with a fork and let stand, uncovered, 5 to 10 minutes.

For A Change of Pace, Vary The Liquid

Variety is easily obtained by varying the cooking liquid. Try using tomato, or even apple or orange juice. A nice change is provided by using reconstituted chicken or beef soup base. In that case, watch the amount of salt used, for soup bases vary in their saltiness. Thinly sliced chicken wheat meat served in gravy over a bed of rice makes a very satisfying meal for just pennies.

The following recipe comes from Thailand where the art of making a little bit of meat go a long way is practiced. You can utilize leftovers, or cut off a small portion of a roast, etc. to reserve when planning to make this meal at a later date. To cut the meat thinly, it helps to freeze it just until ice crystals form then cut across the grain with a very sharp knife.

Kau Pat

4-5 Cups cooked rice
1 Cup thinly sliced meat, your choice
1 bunch green onions
1 medium yellow or white onion
1 tomato
2 eggs
Soy sauce
MSG (optional)
Cucumber
Fresh lemon wedges or bottled lemon juice
6 Tablespoons vegetable oil (or bacon drippings for added flavor)

Chop the green onions into thin rings and finely mince the tops. Set them aside in separate bowls. Chop the yellow onion into medium-sized pieces and set aside. Slice the meat across the grain into thin slivers, and set aside. Slice the tomato in half, crosswise, and discard the seedy pulp. Chop the remainder into small pieces and set aside.

Heat the fat in the bottom of a wok or large skillet. Stir in the yellow onion and cook until wilted. Add the meat and stir until cooked, (or in the case of leftovers, heated through). Crack the eggs into the pan and stir them until cooked. Add the green onion slices and the cooked rice. To help break up the rice, give several shakes of soy sauce and mix all the ingredients together. Cook over medium heat until hot, then add the minced onion tops (reserving a little for garnish), and the chopped tomato. Sprinkle liberally with MSG, stir and adjust seasoning, adding more soy sauce if needed. Serve at once, or cover and keep warm until serving. Pass around cucumber slices and lemon wedges to be eaten with the rice. Garnish with additional minced green onion tops.

Rice-A-Roonie

2 Cups raw rice
1/2 Cup chopped onion
1/2 Cup dry homemade spaghetti, broken into 1/2″ pieces
4 Tablespoons chicken fat, or butter or margarine
4 1/2 Cups hot chicken or beef stock, or reconstituted soup base
1 Tablespoon dried or minced fresh parsley (optional)

In a large skillet with a tight fitting cover, heat the fat or butter. Add the rice and dry spaghetti, stirring over medium high heat until the pasta is brown and the rice golden. Add the onions and stir until wilted. Add the hot stock and the parsley, stir and cover with the lid. Turn heat to low and cook for 20 to 25 minutes, or until the rice is tender and the liquid absorbed. If it appears to be drying before reaching the tender stage, add a little hot water and cook a little longer. For variety, try adding a few cooked green peas just before serving.

Rice Pudding

3 Cups cooked rice
4 Cups milk, soy milk or Milk♥Lite®
3/4 Cup white or brown sugar
2 Tablespoons butter or margarine
1/2 teaspoon nutmeg or allspice
1/4 teaspoon salt
2 eggs
1/2 Cup raisins
1 teaspoon vanilla

Combine the rice, raisins, sugar, salt and nutmeg or allspice in a large saucepan. Stir in the milk and cook over medium heat until thick and creamy. Stir frequently to prevent scorching. Beat the eggs in a small bowl. Pour, while stirring, a small amount of the hot pudding into the beaten eggs, then stir the egg mixture back into the pudding. Cook and stir for about three more minutes. Add the butter and vanilla and serve either warm or chilled. For variety, we suggest a little grated orange rind in place of the nutmeg.

Oats

Oat grain is enjoying a high level of popularity today, with much publicity being ascribed to the value of its bran in the reduction of cholesterol. This fact, alone would account for its popularity, however, there is much more to the oat than bran.

Oats are the only grain that go through processing without losing any of their nutritive value. They are easy to prepare, easy to digest, and easy to love for their culinary adaptability. Possessing a bland flavor, they go well in desserts, cookies, breads, main dishes, and the ever-popular breakfast cereals.

How We Can Use Oats

Oat flour is easily made at home, either in a blender, food processor, or grain mill. Because the oat is a soft grain, it is better NOT to use a stone grinder which could be damaged by the clogging of the stone's pores. Oat flour can be used as a direct substitute for wheat flour in the thickening of stews, puddings, gravies, sauces and soups. When used to replace up to 1/3 of the flour in any recipe, oat flour imparts moistness, nutrition, and prolongs freshness.

Most of us, when thinking of oats, picture the familiar rolled form. But in addition to rolled oats and oat flour, the grain is available in groat form (the whole kernel from which the hull has been removed); steel cut (cut or broken into several pieces for quicker cooking similar to cracked wheat); and quick oats (like the rolled oats, but flatter and more quickly cooked).

Oat Crunch

Make up a batch of this crunchy oat topping and keep it in the refrigerator for use at a moment's notice. The savory variation makes a delicious substitute for bread crumbs or croutons in salads, casseroles or soups, while the sweet version is a perfect topper to ice cream, puddings, desserts, and homemade yogurt.

Savory version:

2½ Cups rolled or quick oats
1/2 Cup grated Parmesan cheese
2/3 Cup margarine or butter
1/4 Cup wheat germ or bran (left from wheat meat washing)
1/4 teaspoon garlic powder
1/4 teaspoon onion powder
1/4 teaspoon salt

In a large saucepan, melt the butter or margarine. Stir in the remaining ingredients, mixing well. Turn out on an ungreased large baking pan and bake in a 350° oven for about 15 minutes or until golden brown. Stir periodically to prevent scorching. Store, tightly covered, in the refrigerator.

Sweet version:

1¾ Cups rolled or quick oats
1/2 teaspoon cinnamon
1/3 Cup wheat germ or bran (left from wheat meat washing)
1/2 Cup brown sugar, packed
1/2 Cup margarine or butter

In a large skillet, melt the butter or margarine. Add the remaining ingredients and mix well. Stirring constantly, cook over medium heat until golden brown, about 5 minutes. Spread out on clean surface and cool thoroughly before storing, tightly covered, in the refrigerator.

Granola

Where would we be without granola? It's a little like a folk song: everyone has a different verse, or version. Here's one we think you'll like.

3 Cups rolled oats
1/3 Cup wheat germ
1/3 Cup honey or corn syrup
1/2 teaspoon salt
1 Cup soy nuts (See Snack section)
1/3 Cup butter or margarine
1/3 Cup brown sugar, packed
1½ teaspoon cinnamon
1 Cup raisins

In a large bowl, mix together all the dry ingredients except raisins and soy nuts. In a small pan, melt the butter and stir in the honey or corn syrup. Pour over the oat mixture and mix well. Place on a large, ungreased baking pan and bake at 350°, stirring frequently for 25 to 30 minutes.

While the mixture is still warm, stir in raisins. When it has cooled, add the soy nuts. Store tightly covered. For variations, add sunflower seeds, sesame seeds, or coconut. This is great by itself as a snack, or as a cereal with milk.

Oatmeal Cake

This cake is so moist that, given the opportunity, it could stay fresh for days, even without frosting. In fact, frosting this cake is truly 'gilding the lily'. All it needs is a sprinkling of **OAT CRUNCH** prior to baking.

This cake travels well to potlucks, picnics and other get-togethers.

Oatmeal Cake (Continued)

$2^1/_2$ Cups boiling water
2 Cups rolled oats
2 Cups brown sugar
2 Cups white sugar
1 Cup butter or margarine
4 eggs
2 teaspoons soda
2 teaspoons cinnamon
1 teaspoon salt
$2^2/_3$ Cups unbleached flour

In a medium-sized bowl, pour the boiling water over the oats and let stand 20 minutes. Meanwhile, melt the butter or margarine in a small pan and, when cooled somewhat, beat in the eggs. Mix together the dry ingredients and add along with the butter mixture to the soaked oats. Stir well and pour into a greased 9″ x 13″ baking pan. Bake at 350° for about one hour, or until a toothpick probe comes out clean. This needs no frosting, but if desired, sprinkle with OAT CRUNCH before baking. This recipe can be halved, in which case the baking time is reduced to 30 to 35 minutes.

Meatballs In Gravy

This recipe underscores the versatility of oats. They impart a good texture and increase the nutrition of this homey dish.

$1^1/_2$ Pounds ground beef
1 Cup rolled oats
2 eggs
1 teaspoon seasoned salt
1/4 Cup tomato sauce or catsup
2 teaspoons soy sauce
1 teaspoon rubbed or ground sage
1/2 teaspoon pepper
1 small onion, chopped fine
2 Cups mushroom soup (See Soup Section)

In a large bowl, combine all the ingredients except the soup. Form into balls the size of golf balls and brown in a large skillet lightly greased with vegetable oil. Turn heat to medium and pour the soup over. Cover and cook for about 20 to 30 minutes. Serve over pasta or rice. Serves 6 to 8.

Rye

Rye is one of the most important grains of northern Europe, where it thrives in the cold, damp climate. Tolerating rocky, infertile soils where other grains won't grow, it yields an abundant, nutritious crop.

Producing a very dark flour with much lower gluten content than wheat, rye gives the typical dark, heavy character to Northern Europe's breads.

Although we generally think of rye in terms of bread, it is also valuable as a livestock feed, important in the making of whiskey, and delicious in muffins, cookies, pancakes, and even pie crust. It can be enjoyed as a cooked cereal in either its whole form, or cracked. Rye is also tasty as pilaf, in casseroles, or, when sprouted, in salads.

When used in bread making, rye is most often blended with wheat flour to yield a lighter textured loaf. Although an all-rye loaf can be made, the usual ratio is 2 parts rye to 5 parts wheat flour.

Pumpernickel Rye Bread

3 Tablespoons or pkgs. dry yeast
2 1/2 Tablespoons vegetable oil
1 1/2 Cups lukewarm water
3-3 1/2 Cups unbleached flour
1/2 Cup molasses
3 teaspoons salt
3 1/4 Cups rye flour
2 teaspoons caraway seeds

In a large bowl, dissolve the yeast in the water. When thoroughly dissolved, beat in all remaining ingredients except the white flour. Add the white, or unbleached, flour gradually until the dough is stiff and pulls away from the sides of the bowl. Turn out on lightly floured counter and knead until smooth. Place in greased bowl, turning over to grease the top, and cover the dough with plastic. Let rise until doubled. Divide in half and form each piece into a round ball. Place each in a greased cake pan and cover again. Let rise until almost double, then bake at 375° for 40 to 45 minutes. Cool on a wire rack. Makes 2 loaves.

Rye Pie Pastry

2 Cups rye flour
1/2 teaspoon salt
2/3 Cup shortening
4-5 Tablespoons ice water

Sift and measure flour into a medium bowl. Stir in the salt. With pastry blender, or two knives, cut in 1/3 Cup of the shortening until mixture has the consistency of cornmeal. Cut in the remaining shortening until it is the size

Rye Pie Pastry (Continued)

of peas. (The first makes for tenderness, the second for flakiness.) With a fork, gently stir in the ice water and push ingredients together into a ball. Press together and cut in half. Roll out between sheets of waxed paper until the crust extends 1 inch beyond the edge of the pan, taking care as crust is fragile. If making a two-crust pie, add filling, then top with second crust, fold under and flute. Cut vents in the top crust and bake, per filling instructions. For single crusts, fold under edge of crust and flute. Prick with a fork and bake at 425° for 10 to 12 minutes.

Rye/Berry Pie

5 Cups berries of your choice (Strawberries are good)
1 Cup granulated sugar
3½ Tablespoons corn starch
2 Tablespoons lemon juice
4 Tablespoons powdered sugar
1 baked rye pie shell

Mash 2 Cups of berries in a medium saucepan. Mix 1 Cup granulated sugar with cornstarch and add to berries in pan. Cook, stirring, over medium heat and add lemon juice. Let cool. Sprinkle powdered sugar over crust and fill with fresh whole berries. Pour mashed berry mixture over and chill before serving.

Barley

It is believed the foxtail, that annoying weed that sticks to socks and slacks, was the foundation grass for the development of this most useful grain. (Who says there isn't a purpose for everything!)

Containing no gluten, barley makes a poor bread by itself. However, a little barley flour added to pastries or whole grain breads helps to ensure a lighter product. For every cup, substitute 2 Tablespoons of barley flour for 2 Tablespoons of wheat flour. (Barley flour, we should point out, is easily made in any grain mill.)

Anyone who enjoys the flavor of malt is indebted to barley. It is made by steeping seed barley, or sprouting barley, in warm water. (Pearled, or processed, barley won't sprout.) It is then sprouted, dried, cracked with a rolling pin, and roasted in the oven to the desired shade and flavor, after which it is ground to a powder. Barley is very easy to digest and so finds favor as a good source of nourishment for invalids in the form of hot broth, or tea.

Barley Water or Tea

Soak 1 Tablespoon barley overnight in 3 Cups water to soften. Next day, bring to a boil and simmer until barley is tender. Strain and salt to taste.

Barley Soup

1 Medium onion, chopped
1 clove garlic, minced
1/2 Cup barley
7 Cups water
1/2 teaspoon dry sweet basil
1/2 Cup sliced carrots
2 medium potatoes, cubed
1/2 Cup sliced celery
2 small bay leaves
3 teaspoons beef soup base
1 quart homecanned tomatoes, <u>or</u> 1 large can whole tomatoes
2 Tablespoons vegetable oil or margarine

In the bottom of a large pot, cook the onions and garlic in the oil or margarine until wilted. Add the remaining ingredients and simmer over low heat about 1 hour. If soup becomes too thick after standing, add additional water. Serves about 12.

Millet

Although thought of primarily as birdseed in the United States, millet is an ancient cereal grain, cultivated and enjoyed by over a third of the world's population for thousands of years. It is characterized by a sweet, mild flavor and is delicious when used as a change from rice. An easily digested, most nutritious cereal, millet certainly deserves a greater place in our modern diets. Here are a few recipes to help you get better acquainted with this golden grain.

Hot Cooked Millet

Boil millet in an uncovered pan for 30 to 35 minutes, adding water as needed. Or measure 1 part millet to 2 parts water and simmer, covered, 30 to 35 minutes. Add 1/2 teaspoon salt per each 1/2 Cup of millet used. With the addition of milk and butter, or sugar, this makes a delicious hot cereal for breakfast, or it can substitute in any recipe which calls for hot cooked rice.

Millet Puff

2 Cups cooked millet
3/4 Cup milk, soy milk or Milk♥Lite®
1/2 Cup shredded homemade Colby or Jack cheese
4 eggs, separated
1 teaspoon salt

Beat the egg yolks in a medium sized bowl until thick. Stir in the cooked millet, salt, milk, and all but 2 Tablespoons of the cheese. Beat the egg whites until stiff and gently fold into the mixed ingredients. Pour into a 6-Cup, ungreased oven-proof dish and sprinkle with the remaining cheese. Bake at 375° for about 30 minutes, or until a knife inserted in the center comes out clean. Serves 4 to 6.

Fried Millet

1¼ Cups millet
3/4 Cup shredded homemade cheese
4 scant teaspoons chicken or beef soup base
3 Tablespoons lard or vegetable oil
4 Tablespoons butter or margarine
3¾ Cups boiling water
1 large onion

Slice the onion very thinly into rings. Cook until limp in the oil or lard using a large skillet with a lid. Add the millet and cook, stirring constantly, about 3 to 4 minutes. Dissolve the soup base in the boiling water and add to the millet/onion mixture in the pan. Cook over medium heat for 18 to 20 minutes, stirring frequently. Taste test for tenderness. Stir in the butter and cheese and cover for 5 minutes. Fluff with a fork before serving. Serves 4.

Dried Beans

Beans have been grown the world over for generations. They are generally thought of as peasant fare, being easily grown and stored, inexpensive, nutritious and filling. Many a family throughout history has owed its winter survival to a larder stocked with beans.

While not a complete protein in themselves, beans are full of nutrition. The incomplete protein found in beans is made complete by the pairing of beans with animal proteins such as meat, cheese, or milk. Traditionally, most of the favorite dishes utilizing beans find them just so combined.

The bargain value of beans is apparent when one realizes that it takes only one quarter cup to make one serving, or that one pound of beans will feed seven to nine people.

Hundreds of varieties of dried beans and related legumes are available in all imaginable shapes, colors and sizes. Different locales have different favorites and beans are fun to experiment with.

To Cook Dry Beans

1. Sort through the beans, removing any rocks.
2. Rinse and cover with water in a pan large enough to allow the beans to double in size.
3. Bring to a boil and continue boiling for two minutes. Then either:
   a) Soak overnight for cooking the next day. (The initial two minute boiling period prevents their souring.)
   b) Soak one hour in the same water. Resume cooking in the same water or, to lessen the infamous gas-producing quality of beans, use fresh water for the cooking.
4. Be sure the beans are completely covered with water during the entire cooking time, which should take from 1 to 3 hours.

Tips On Bean Cookery

1. Use the softest water possible. Hard water toughens beans. To soften hard water, first boil the water vigorously for 20 to 30 minutes in a tightly covered container. This will precipitate some of the hard water salts which toughen the beans.
2. Wait to add salt until just before the beans are tender, about 30 minutes before the cooking time is up.

3. If adding tomatoes, catsup or vinegar, wait until the beans have softened, because these acids, if added earlier, would delay the softening.
4. Avoid over-cooking. Beans actually become tougher when overdone. A well-cooked bean has a tender skin and a somewhat mealy texture.
5. Boil gently and avoid over stirring to keep the beans intact.
6. If baking beans, use an oven temperature of no higher than 325°. A higher temperature increases the evaporation, resulting in a greater concentration of salt, and therefore a tougher bean.

Although plain, boiled beans are delicious in themselves, here are a few speedy tricks you can use to dress them up:

- Try seasoning cooked, drained beans with butter, margarine, bacon fat, or other meat drippings
- To the above, add finely minced green pepper or celery.
- Add to drained beans finely chopped onions and a speedy sauce made by thinning catsup or chili sauce with some of the bean liquor (cooking liquid).
- For an inexpensive "cheese flavor" stir in slowly to each cup of drained, cooked pinto or pink beans, 1/3 Cup dry powdered milk. Serve on corn or flour tortillas with chopped onion.

Sprouting Mung Beans

An almost indispensable ingredient in Oriental cookery, bean sprouts give foods a delicious crunchy texture, not to mention a vitamin boost. Using a slightly different technique from that used in other sprouting, they are easy to grow.

1. Swish the beans in a pan of warm water, discarding those that float. Soak in tepid water 18-24 hours, changing water if it sours.
2. Drain and place in a colander, covering with a double thickness of cheesecloth. Place a weight on the cloth: a brick, gallon jug of water, or whatever you can improvise.
3. Keep the beans at room temperature, rinsing them three times daily by running water through the colander, disturbing them as little as possible.
4. In anywhere from 5 days to a week, the bean sprouts should reach 4 inches in length and, when rinsed thoroughly in cold water, should be ready for use. Stored in a damp paper towel in the crisper of your refrigerator, they will keep fresh and crisp for several days.

Baked Beans

2 pounds navy or pea beans
12 Cups cold water
1 large onion
3/4 pound salt pork
1/2 Cup brown sugar
1 teaspoon dry mustard
1/4 teaspoon ground cloves
1/4 teaspoon ground ginger
2 teaspoons salt
1 Cup boiling water

Wash and pick over the beans. Cover with the cold water and bring to a boil. Boil 2 minutes, then cover and remove from heat. Let stand for 1 hour. Simmer over low heat until the skins burst when blown upon in a spoon. Drain and place in an oven-proof bean pot with the whole onion. Briefly scald the salt pork in water to cover (this will remove some of the excess salt). Score the rind with cuts about every 1/2 inch, and make them 1 inch deep. Bury the salt pork in the beans, leaving the rind exposed. Mix the brown sugar with the spices and boiling water and pour over the beans and pork. If beans are not covered, add a little water. Cover and bake in a slow oven, 250° or overnight, adding more water as needed. Next day, uncover and bake 30 more minutes until a crust forms. Serves 10 to 12.

Refritos I (Refried Beans)

Unfortunately, these refritos will never qualify as a diet dish. The thing that gives them the authentic flavor is the fat used in preparation.

1 pound pink, pinto, or kidney beans
1/2 Cup or more (!) bacon drippings
1 teaspoon salt
1½ quarts water

Sort and cook the beans (See cooking instructions) with the water, add salt. In a large heavy skillet, heat the bacon fat. Scoop the beans from the cooking liquid into the pan and mash them in the fat. Do this a little at a time, mashing after each addition and stirring constantly. If you prefer, put drained beans in a blender or ricer and blend until smooth. Cook the bean mixture in the skillet, scraping the bottom to keep from burning, until the consistency is thick and the fat is absorbed. Sometimes a little reserved bean liquor can be added to adjust the consistency. Refritos are exceptionally delicious if a cup or two of shredded homemade Monterey Jack or Colby cheese is stirred in just before serving. This freezes well.

Refritos II (Refried Beans)

Fortunately, these refritos CAN qualify as a diet dish, so now everybody can be happy. (If they could just do the same for a Danish!)

Refritos II (Refried Beans), Continued

2 Cups presoaked beans, pintos, pink or kidney*
1 Tablespoon beef or ham soup base
1 medium onion, chopped
1 whole, intact green pepper
1 jalapeño pepper, minced
6-6 1/2 Cups water
salt and pepper to taste

* See cooking instructions for beans on Page 84

In a large saucepan, cook all the ingredients but salt until the beans are tender. Add salt to taste during the last few cooking minutes. Drain and reserve the cooking liquid, if any remains. Place all in a blender and whirl until smooth, adding liquid if needed for desired consistency. Adjust salt and pepper and serve while hot.

Bean Fudge (!)

1 Cup soft cooked pinto or pink beans
1/4-1/2 Cup milk, soy milk or Milk♥Lite®
6 Squares unsweetened chocolate
1 Tablespoon vanilla
6 Tablespoons butter or margarine
2 pounds powdered sugar

In a medium-sized bowl, mash together the beans and vanilla. Add enough milk to produce the consistency of mashed potatoes. Melt the butter and chocolate over low heat and mix into the bean mixture. Stir until it thickens slightly. With a wooden spoon, or hands, work in the powdered sugar. Press into buttered pan. Makes about 3 1/2 pounds.

Bind It Together Or Dress It Up

(Featuring Sauces, Dressings and Condiments)

As the title suggests, this chapter provides recipes to enhance, or hold together the dishes you create. The word "sauce" is derived from the Latin, "salsus", meaning "flavored with salt". The sauces of those days were well named, for most were concocted from salted, fermented fish. Until the end of the Middle Ages, sauces served mainly to disguise the taste of meat that was tainted from non-refrigeration.

Why sauces?

Today, however, sauces are used to complement or blend the flavors in a particular dish. In some cases, as in the use of wheat meat, they are essential to carry off the delightful deception, causing people to think they are eating the genuine article.

Here are some favorite ones often refered to in this book. With practice you'll find it's easier and tastier to create your own than to open an expensive can. Most freeze well, so it is a simple matter to thaw a block of sauce when you need it.

Red Enchilada Sauce (Mild Flavored)

This, and the sauce that follows, are the two sauces we use in the making of wheat meat burritos and chimichangas. This sauce is also good for enchiladas and with eggs in ranchos huevos. It can be made hotter, if desired, by adding a pinch of chile tepines, or tabasco. The best flavor is achieved by the use of lard, but vegetable oil can be substituted.

1/2 Cup vegetable oil or lard
1 medium onion, chopped
1 clove garlic, minced
1/2 Cup flour
2 Tablespoons sugar
salt/pepper to taste
2 Tablespoons chili powder
3-4 Cups homemade tomato sauce
3-4 Cups water
2 teaspoons vinegar

Melt the fat in a large saucepan. Add the onion and garlic and cook until translucent. Stir in the flour until smooth and thick. Add the tomato sauce and water and the remaining ingredients. Mix well and reduce heat to as low as possible. Cook covered until flavors blend, about 1 hour. It freezes well and keeps, refrigerated, for up to two weeks.

Thick Green Sauce

6 Tablespoons vegetable shortening (or bacon drippings, best flavor)
1/2 Cup chopped roasted, peeled green chiles (3-4 whole)
1/2 Cup flour
1/2 Cup chopped onion
3 1/2 teaspoons beef soup base
2 Cups water
1 teaspoon ground cumin, (comino)

Melt the fat in a small saucepan. Sauté the onion until clear, then add the soup base. Stir to dissolve, then blend in the flour.

Add the remaining ingredients and cook over low heat until smooth and thick. Use as is in burritos, or thin with a little water to use with tacos, etc. Freezes well.

Hot Chinese Mustard

Make a soupy paste of dry mustard powder and water. Let stand 10 minutes before using to let flavor develop. Use with caution, for a little goes a **LONG** way!

Sweet and Sour Sauce

Mix 1/2 Cup brown sugar with 2 Tablespoons cornstarch. Add 1/2 Cup vinegar and 1 1/2 Cups homemade catsup. Cook over low heat, stirring constantly until thickened.

Homemade Tomato Sauce

Indispensable to many recipes, this recipe makes 8 pints you can bottle, or freeze. It also keeps several weeks in the refrigerator, tightly covered.

12-15 Pounds fresh tomatoes
4 large onions, chopped
2 cloves minced garlic
4 stalks celery, chopped
3 large bell peppers, chopped
1 Tablespoon oregano
2 teaspoons vinegar
4 Tablespoons brown sugar
1 Tablespoon sweet basil
1 Tablespoon salt
2 Tablespoons fresh minced, or dried parsley
Several twists fresh ground pepper

Wash the tomatoes well, core and remove any blemishes. Peel by dipping briefly in boiling water and slipping the skins. Chop and put in large, heavy pot, or large roasting pan. Cook over low heat, or in the oven on low (200° to 250°) for two hours or so. Stir often, if using the stove top method, to prevent scorching. Add remaining ingredients, and cook overnight, or until as thick as you desire. Whirl in a blender or put through a food processor for a smooth sauce. Can in pint or quart jars, **using only a Pressure Canner** at 10 lbs pressure, 20 minutes for pints, 25 minutes for quarts. If desired, freeze.

Jenny's Spaghetti Sauce

4 Cups homemade tomato sauce
3 twists fresh ground pepper
1/2 Cup chopped onion
1 teaspoon beef soup base, or to taste
1/4 Cup homemade Parmesan, grated
2 teaspoons butter or margarine
1 teaspoon garlic powder
4 teaspoons sugar
2 teaspoons sweet basil
2 teaspoons oregano
1/4 Cup red wine (optional)

In large saucepan sauté all the ingredients except Parmesan, tomato sauce & wine. Stir well and when onion is wilted, add tomato sauce and wine. Simmer for at least an hour to blend the flavors. Add the cheese and cook until melted and smooth.

Prepared Mustard

2/3 Cup vinegar
1/3 Cup butter or margarine
1½ teaspoons salt
1 large egg or 2 small ones
1½-2 teaspoons turmeric
1/4 Cup sugar
1/2 Cup water
2/3 Cup flour
3/4 teaspoon dry mustard

Put the ingredients in a blender and whirl until smooth. Pour into a medium saucepan and cook over medium heat until thick and smooth. Stir constantly to keep from scorching. Pour into a glass jar and cap tightly. Keep refrigerated.

Tomato Catsup

1/4 Cup vinegar
1/2 teaspoon cinnamon
1/4 teaspoon ground cloves
1/2 teaspoon celery seed
1/8 teaspoon cayenne pepper
6 large ripe tomatoes
4 Tablespoons brown sugar
1 teaspoon salt
1/3 Cup minced onion
1/2 Cup water

Peel tomatoes and remove cores. Cut into pieces and place in heavy pot with onion and water. Cook until soft and put through blender until smooth. Add remaining ingredients and cook over low heat, stirring to prevent scorching, until the desired consistency is reached. This could take two hours or more. Store, tightly covered, in the refrigerator.

Tartar Sauce

1 Cup homemade mayonnaise
1/4 teaspoon dry mustard
4 teaspoons lemon juice
1/4 teaspoon celery seed (optional)
4 Tablespoons finely minced sweet or dill pickle
1 Tablespoon finely minced onion

Blend ingredients and chill at least one hour. Serve with fish or wheat meat fish strips or shrimp.

Salsa Fria

(This is good with chips, tacos, quesadillas, etc.)

1 medium onion OR 8 little green onions including tops, chopped
1 chopped, roasted peeled green chile **1 clove garlic, minced**
5 large tomatoes, peeled & chopped **$1\frac{1}{2}$ Tablespoons vinegar**
2 Tablespoons chopped fresh cilantro **1 Tablespoon vegetable oil**

Mix ingredients together. Chill. Keep refrigerated.

Seafood Cocktail Sauce

This is good on seafood or any fish. We serve this sauce with our wheat meat shrimp and no one knows they aren't the "Real McCoy".

3 Tablespoons catsup **3 drops Tabasco sauce** (optional)
1/2 Tablespoon lemon juice **pinch of salt** (optional)
1 teaspoon prepared, OR 1/2 teaspoon fresh horseradish, grated

Combine ingredients, mix well. Keep refrigerated.

Ranch Type Salad Dressing

$1\frac{1}{2}$ Cups mayonnaise **3 Tablespoons sugar**
$2\frac{1}{2}$ Cups cultured buttermilk **2 Tablespoons vinegar**
1 Tablespoon garlic powder **2 Tablespoons parsley flakes**
1 Tablespoon onion powder **Salt, to taste**

Mix all together in a small bowl and keep tightly covered in the refrigerator.

Barbecue sauce

1/2 Cup catsup **1/3 Cup sugar**
1 onion, minced **1/3 Cup vinegar**
1 Tablespoon Worcestershire Sauce **1 teaspoon salt**
1/4 teaspoon garlic powder **Tabasco sauce (to taste)**

Mix all ingredients together in a medium saucepan and simmer for 10 minutes. Keep refrigerated in a tightly closed container.

Mayonnaise

2 teaspoons salt **2 Cups salad oil**
2 Egg yolks **2 teaspoons powdered sugar**
A dash of cayenne pepper **1teaspoon dry mustard**
1/4 Cup homemade vinegar or lemon juice

Combine dry ingredients in a bowl with the unbeaten yolks and beat together until stiff. While beating vigorously, start adding the oil, drop by drop. Increase the amount of oil as you continue beating, keeping the mixture stiff. When it begins to thicken, add the vinegar or lemon juice alternately with the oil until blended. Chill before using. Makes about $2\frac{1}{2}$ Cups.

Sumptuous Snacks, Soups and Sandwiches

Our program depends heavily upon the ability to make most of the staples we use. This, as you realize, creates a great savings. One of the areas in the food budget that seems to take the biggest bite with apparently the least return is in the snack department. It is difficult to say NO! with all the latest offerings screaming at you from the well-stocked supermarket shelves. With this section, no one needs feel deprived, for easy-to-make treats are at your fingertips. This all helps to keep within the $10 a week plan.

SNACKS

"Falcon Brand" Peanut-Granola Balls

1½ Cups homemade sweetened condensed milk (See index)
1 Cup peanut butter (may be extended with soy , See index)
3 Cups granola (See index)

Mix all the ingredients together and roll into balls the size of walnuts. Store, tightly covered, in the refrigerator. Makes about 50.

Banana-Yogurt Frozen Cups

1/2 Cup homemade plain or vanilla yogurt
1/3 Cup milk, soy milk or Milk♥Lite®
1½ Tablespoons sugar or honey
3 small bananas
1/2 teaspoon vanilla

Put all the ingredients in the blender and whirl until smooth. Pour into 6 paper cups and freeze until mushy. Insert a popsicle stick into each and freeze solid.

Cheesy Potato Snacks

4-6 small potatoes
1/3 Cup Parmesan cheese, grated
1½ Tablespoons melted butter or margarine

Scrub potatoes but do not peel. Slice thinly and place in a thin layer on greased cookie sheets. Spread with the melted butter and sprinkle with the cheese. Grate a little fresh pepper over the top. Bake in a 450° oven for 20 minutes until they are crispy brown. Serves 6.

Soy "Nuts"

Soak soybeans overnight. Rinse and pat dry. Heat vegetable oil to 375° and add soybeans, no more than 1 Cup at a time. Cook until golden brown. Drain on a paper towel and salt, if desired.

Use in place of nuts in recipes, or as a snack. For a real treat, dip in melted chocolate or use melted white dipping confection.

Garlic Tofu Dip

1/2 Pound tofu (See Soybean section)
1 Tablespoon honey
2 Tablespoons lemon juice
1 clove garlic, finely minced
3 Tablespoons cream cheese (optional)
1 Tablespoon oil
1½ cloves garlic
1/2 teaspoon garlic powder
3/4 teaspoon salt

Put tofu, oil, lemon juice, 1½ cloves garlic, salt and cream cheese in blender. Whirl until smooth and creamy. Stir in the garlic powder, honey and minced garlic clove. Makes about 1½ Cups.

This may seem like a lot of garlic, but it is delicious with fresh, crisp vegetables or homemade crackers.

SOUP

Basic to almost every good soup is a stock, preferably homemade. It is so important, in fact, that in France it goes by the name of "fond", as in foundation.

Stocking Up on Stock

Stock making is economical, for the long, slow cooking extracts the very essence of the vegetables used. Anything and everything goes into the stock pot; nothing is wasted. Well washed potato peelings and carrot scrapings, wilted vegetables lost in the back of the refrigerator crisper, a smidgen of leftovers from a previous dinner - all contribute to the heartiness of the stock.

Modern day technology makes it easy to collect the makings of a good stock, for a plastic bag kept in the freezer provides a good receptacle while the "goodies" accumulate. Don't overlook onion skins, for their addition to the pot helps to give a deep, rich color. When ready to start, use one and a half to two times the amount of water to the amount of vegetables.

In a generation not too far removed from today, the "back of the stove" was an ideal location for bread raising, cheese making, keeping food warm and for stock making. The temperature there was even and gentle. Many of our pots today lack the heavy weight needed to prevent scorching when long, unattended cooking is required. A simple way to overcome this problem is to place the pot on two or three bricks placed on the burner. Arrange them so they support the pot from the edges, leaving the center free. Another solution is found in the use of a slow cooker. When left overnight to its own devices, the result the next morning is a fragrant kitchen and vegetables ready for the next step:

Reserve the cooking water and put the vegetables in a ricer or food mill. In some instances a blender is helpful, but in this case the pureé needs to be separated from the fibrous matter and a ricer is the better choice. Discard the pulp and combine the pureé with the cooking water. What was once scraps and leftovers now is vegetable stock, with very little effort on your part.

"Free Meal" Soup

This stock can be frozen or used now for soup. The character of the soup is left to the cook's discretion. Additional vegetables are added, perhaps some garlic and a bay leaf to boost the seasoning, although with a hearty stock it is not essential. If desired, pieces of meat, well browned in a skillet, may be added. Bones, previously browned in the oven, when added to the soup lend color and flavor at no cost.

The resulting soup can be considered a free dinner and is so hearty and filling you will be anxious to begin collecting leftovers all over again.

Cream of Mushroom

Basic to many of the recipes in this book, this soup is delicious just by itself, accompanied by one of the cracker recipes found in the Wheat Section.

2 Cups milk, soy milk or Milk♥Lite®
3/4 Cup flour
3 Tablespoons butter or margarine
3/4 teaspoon seasoned salt (See index)
A twist fresh ground pepper

Blend the above until smooth, then cook over medium heat until thickened. Blend in, a little at a time,

Add:

1 Cup additional milk, soy milk or Milk♥Lite®
1½ Cups chicken broth **1/4 teaspoon garlic powder**
1/2 teaspoon onion powder **1/2 teaspoon ground thyme**
1 Cup fresh mushrooms chopped fine, sautéed in 2 Tablespoons of butter, OR
1 4-ounce can undrained mushrooms, chopped fine

Heat through, but do not allow to boil. Thin with milk if it seems too thick.

"In A Minute" Cream Soup

Toss leftover vegetables such as spinach, peas, cauliflower, or carrots into the blender with 1 cup chicken broth and 1/2 Cup undiluted canned milk. Blend, season with curry powder or Worcestershire and. . . Instant soup.

French Onion Soup

1 Quart beef stock or bouillon or reconstituted beef soup base
3½ Cups thinly sliced yellow or white onions
6 thick slices French bread (or see Baguettes in Bread Section)
Homemade Parmesan cheese, grated
1/4 Cup butter or margarine
2 Tablespoons flour
1/2 teaspoon salt (watch amount)
4 Tablespoons sugar

Sauté onion slices in butter in a large skillet. Cover and cook for 10 to 15 minutes. Add sugar, flour, and salt. Stir. Combine with the beef stock in a large pot and cook over low heat 2 to 3 hours, (Covered). To serve: Ladle into bowls and top with a slice of the French bread, upon which has been sprinkled Parmesan cheese. Serves 6.

SANDWICHES

P. B. Rarebit

3/4 Cup milk, soy milk or Milk♥Lite®
2 slices toast
1 Egg
1/2 teaspoon salt
3 Tablespoons peanut butter

In the top of a double boiler, beat the egg. Stir in the milk, salt, and peanut butter. Cook until smooth, about 10 to 12 minutes. Spoon over buttered toast. Serves 2.

Puffy Burgers

3 hot fried wheat meat hamburger patties (See Wheat Meat)
Homemade mayonnaise
1 egg white
3 tomato slices
3 onion slices
3 slices toast

Beat egg whites until stiff and fold in the mayonnaise. Spread each slice of toast with additional mayonnaise and top with a patty, slice of onion and slice of tomato. Mound egg white mixture on top and brown lightly in a 400° oven for 8 to 10 minutes. Makes 3.

Mock Chicken Salad (Or Beef, or Ham)

1 Wheat Meat roast, 4″ x 2½″, chicken, beef or ham flavored
1 Tablespoon chopped celery
1 Tablespoon finely minced onion
Mayonnaise, to taste (See index)
Chopped black olives (optional)
Chopped pickles or pickle relish, to taste (optional)

Grind the cooked roast in a food grinder. You should have approximately 1½ cups. Mix with the remaining ingredients and adjust for personal preferences. Serve on split biscuits or buns, garnished, if desired, with a whole black olive skewered on a cocktail pick.

"Lunchmeat"

Make one recipe raw gluten. (See Wheat Meat Section for directions)

Roll and stretch to 1/4″ thickness. Sprinkle with 1 teaspoon each ham and beef soup base. Sprinkle with stuffed green olives, or whole black olives; fresh ground pepper or whole peppercorns; pimientos, or pickles, if desired. Roll up tightly in a 2½ inch diameter roll. Either: (1) wrap tightly in foil and simmer in water overnight then unwrap and simmer in broth 2 to 4 hours, or (2) wrap tightly in cloth and secure both ends with string. Simmer in broth 8 to 12 hours. BROTH = 2 Tablespoons ham soup base and 1 Tablespoon beef soup base in 2 quarts of water. Remove from broth, chill and slice thinly.

Quesadillas

Place lightly buttered homemade flour tortillas, (See index) on an ungreased baking sheet. Sprinkle generously with shredded homemade Colby, Jack or Cheddar cheese. Sprinkle with chopped onion, if desired. Toast under broiler until cheese is bubbly and the edges crisp. Serve, if desired, with your favorite salsa or red enchilada sauce **(See index)**

Satisfying the Sweet Tooth

Living our way of life on this program certainly doesn't mean austerity. We don't overlook the need for affordable, delicious goodies. Everyone needs a "warm fuzzy" once in awhile and this chapter has just that. Here are a few of our favorites, from deceptively low fat and calorie-conscious, to frankly and unabashedly decadent. Enjoy!

Olé Apple Strudel

This easy recipe gives the same crispy taste found in traditional strudel that takes hours to prepare. Your homemade tortillas replace the tedious stretching required of the traditional dough.

12 large homemade flour tortillas (see Index)
8-9 tart apples
2 teaspoons ground cinnamon
2/3 Cup butter or margarine, melted
1/2 Cup crushed corn flakes or homemade granola
3/4 Cup raisins
2/3 Cup sugar

Peel and core the apples. Chop finely and mix with the sugar and cinnamon. Add the raisins and set aside. Using a pastry brush, spread a tortilla with melted butter. Sprinkle with crushed cereal and spread with some of the chopped apple mixture. Fold bottom of the tortilla 1/3 over the filling and brush with butter. Fold in both sides and once again, brush with butter. Roll up and brush the outside with the butter. Repeat with all the tortillas. Bake in 350° oven until crispy. Makes 12, and they freeze beautifully.

Custard Crumb Pudding

1 quart milk, soy milk or Milk♥Lite®
2 Cups soft crumbs (stale cake is good)
2 eggs, slightly beaten
1/4 Cup butter or margarine, melted
1/2 teaspoon salt
1 teaspoon vanilla
1/2 Cup sugar
Nutmeg, or allspice

Scald the milk and add the crumbs. Combine eggs, sugar and salt in a 1 1/2 quart baking dish. Mix well, then add the crumb mixture, vanilla and butter. Stir and sprinkle top with nutmeg or allspice. Set bowl in a pan of hot water in the oven and bake 350° for 1 hour or until a knife inserted in the side comes out clean.

Carrot Pie

Although reminiscent of pumpkin, this pie is tasty and delicious all year long. Made with your garden's carrots - fresh or frozen - soy milk and possibly your own honey, it is economical, too.

2 Cups mashed cooked carrots
4 beaten eggs
1 Cup honey or brown sugar
3/4 Cup soy milk or Milk♥Lite®
1/2 teaspoon salt
1/2 teaspoon powdered ginger
1/4 teaspoon ground cloves
1 teaspoon cinnamon
3/4 teaspoon nutmeg (scant)
1 unbaked 9″ pie crust

Blend all the ingredients together until smooth. Pour into pie crust and bake at 400° for 40 to 45 minutes. Garnish with whipped soy topping **(See Soybean Section under "richer milk")** and sprigs of washed carrot tops, if you have them. If not, you can use mint leaves.

Chocolate Wonder Cake

The wonder in this cake is the fact that it's eggless!

3 Cups whole wheat flour*
1/4 Cup mixed oat and barley flour
2 teaspoons baking soda
1 teaspoon salt
2 Tablespoons vinegar
2 Cups water
1½ Cups Sugar
1/2 Cup cocoa
1/2 teaspoon baking powder
2/3 Cup vegetable oil
5 teaspoons vanilla

* Ground from white wheat, available wherever you purchase grain.

Combine the dry ingredients in a large bowl. Mix together the remaining ingredients and stir into the dry mixture. Mix until smooth. Pour into 2 greased and floured 8″ round cake pans. Bake at 350° for 25 to 35 minutes, or until no finger print remains when touched lightly in center.

Buttery Yellow Cake

One of the few homemade cakes that actually has the texture of a mix, the secret lies in the use of barley flour and thorough creaming of the fat, sugar and eggs.

1/4 Cup barley flour*
1 teaspoon baking powder
1/2 teaspoon soda
2 teaspoons vanilla
2 teaspoons butter flavoring(optional)
2¾ Cups sifted flour
4 whole eggs
1 teaspoon salt
2 Cups sugar
1 Cup margarine
1 Cup buttermilk or sour milk (Sour milk by mixing 1 Tablespoon homemade vinegar or lemon juice with 1 cup milk)

* Run barley through mill on fine grind.

Buttery Yellow Cake (Continued)

Sift the dry ingredients together in a small bowl. In a medium mixing bowl beat the margarine and butter flavoring until very light and fluffy. Gradually beat in the sugar, creaming well to dissolve the sugar. Beat in the eggs, one at a time, beating vigorously between each addition. Mix together the buttermilk, or sour milk, with the vanilla and add alternately to the creamed mixture with the sifted dry ingredients. Begin and end with the flour mixture. Blend well, using low speed.

Pour into greased and floured 9″ cake pans if making a conventional layer cake. If making butter sauce cake, pour into a greased and floured 9″ x 13″ baking pan. Bake in 325° oven 40 to 60 minutes, depending upon type pan used. Check for doneness by touching lightly in the center, it will spring back if done. Cool round layers on rack and frost with favorite frosting.

Hot Butter Sauce (if desired):

1 Cup sugar
1/3 Cup water
1/2 Cup butter or margarine
1½ teaspoons vanilla or rum extract

Make butter sauce by heating all ingredients in small saucepan till melted. Prick hot cake all over with a fork and pour the hot butter sauce over the top. Let cool and serve right from the pan.

Produce Your Own Produce

In this program you've seen how each subject, or chapter, intertwines with the others. In this light, you can see how the concept of home gardening is important to our plan of feeding a family of four for as low as $10.00 a week.

That fruits and vegetables are essential to a properly balanced diet, is a well-known fact. What might not be so generally well-known is the fact that it is so easy to grow your own. Not too many years ago, this was the way of life. Every family had a small "kitchen garden". It is an idea that finds merit today, although a number of people seem to lack the confidence to begin. We will show you how easy and relatively chore-free gardening can be.

Gardening is a vast subject and whole books have been written on its various aspects. For the sake of this book, we will focus our attention on container and limited-area gardening and its differences and similarities to conventional gardening.

Who Says You Need A Yard

A large yard, while nice to have, is not an absolute necessity if you desire home-grown produce. A great many plants adapt well to container gardening, and one of the advantages of containers is their mobility. A bare concrete patio, an unsightly corner behind the house, a deck or a balcony, even rooftops—all can be turned into productive garden space with container gardening. Add to that, flower boxes and space usually given over to ornamentals in areas such as walkways and flowerbeds, and your harvest could be fairly substantial.

Soil

Common to both approaches is the need for good soil. While a garden be may be amended to make it suitable for most plants, the same soil would not be successful in a container. When confined in a container, the soil has a tendency to compact, forming a dense mass that neither roots, nor water can penetrate well. This density robs the root hairs of needed oxygen and the plants quite literally drown.

The solution to this problem rests in the use of specially prepared potting soil which is both lightweight, and easy draining. There are many good commercial mixes available, but it is not difficult to mix your own. One simple mix consists of 2 parts garden soil to 1 part sand or vermiculite.

(Vermiculite is an expanded rock, similar in appearance and texture to white mineral Rice Crispies.) Add 1 part leaf mold, compost or peat moss and a little all-purpose fertilizer. Mix well and store in large plastic bags, or in a new plastic garbage pail until ready to use.

Sunlight

Another important factor in the success of a garden is the amount of sunlight it receives. Nearly all garden vegetables prefer a sunny location with at least 6 to 8 hours of sunshine being considered ideal. One of the advantages of container gardening is the ability to shift the plants around to best utilize the available light. You can even create micro-environments for less-sun-loving plants, such as lettuce and spinach, by placing them in the shade created by the taller plants. They frequently benefit from being planted at the base of these plants, saving garden space as a bonus.

Water

Obliviously, water is needed for plant growth, be it in a garden bed or in a container. With container gardening, however, the need is a little more critical. A plant growing in the garden can probe deeply for water and, consequently draw on a greater reserve in times of stress. A container plant is limited by the size of the container, and by its very nature, the container tends to dry out faster. This requires more frequent waterings. The best test is to probe the soil with the finger and if it is dry 2″ below the surface, water. Be especially attentive when the weather is windy, as wind accelerates the drying.

Drainage

As mentioned earlier, good drainage is important. The container should be provided with holes in the bottom, and it helps, when planting, to place a layer of broken clay pottery, or rocks, in the bottom before the potting soil is added. Rocks or bricks placed on the ground serve to raise the container and facilitate drainage. Always use a slow, gentle stream when you water. A forceful stream would dislodge the soil and possibly disturb the roots. If the pot has adequate drainage, the water will emerge from the drainage holes in a matter of minutes. If it stands in puddles on the surface, push a stick through the holes to be sure they are not plugged. If the water gushes through immediately, there is a good chance the potting soil was allowed to get too dry, creating a space between the pot and soil. If this is the case, submerge the entire container in water until the bubbles cease rising. Remove it, allow to drain and try to water more regularly.

MONDA
ROB
WO
Calif
WHITE G
PRODUCED AND BOTTLED BY ROBERT
WOODBRIDGE, CALIFORNIA, PRODUCT

E

F

H

Fertilizing

Having a confined root system causes the plant to depend upon the caretaker for regular feedings. The fertilizer which was mixed with the original potting mix will have been depleted by around two weeks of rapid vegetable growth, for they are heavy feeders. Supplemental feeding with a general all-purpose fertilizer every 2 to 4 weeks is sufficient to carry most plants through to the harvest. For greens and other leafy vegetables, a fertilizer high in nitrogen is preferred.

Always be sure when applying any fertilizer that the soil is moist. Fertilizer applied to dry roots runs the risk of burning them. If you should inadvertently over-fertilize, simply leach the soil by watering until the water has run from the drainage holes for several minutes.

So far we've discussed soil, light requirements, watering, and fertilizing. Still remaining is the question of containers.

Containers

Here is where the imagination rules. Keep in mind the size of the mature plant and plan for ample soil space and adequate drainage. (It might be an obvious point to mention, but if a container fits the requirement, yet lacks the drainage holes, it is a simple matter to drill a few, yourself.)

Planter boxes come in all shapes and sizes and are ideal for nearly anything. Beets and carrots are particularly suited for boxes. Bushel baskets, when filled about one-third with potting mix are perfect for potatoes. Cover the potato pieces (each containing a couple of "eyes"), loosely with the mix and fill the basket with peat as the vines grow. Eventually the basket will be filled with peat and the potatoes are easily lifted from the loose peat in which they develop.

Lettuce makes attractive plantings in clay pots as well as hanging baskets. Swiss chard, particularly the ruby red variety, is a bright visual accent when planted at the base of other plantings. Hanging pots and baskets open up a whole new dimension, for they can be hung anywhere - increasing the garden's size.

Half-barrels and well-cleaned metal drums make fine containers. Even the plastic bag containing potting soil can become a planter with a few drainage holes punched on one side and a slit for the plant on the opposite. Lay the bag on the side and you have a quick mini-garden.

Plastic pails, metal buckets, welded-wire cylinders lined with plastic, old rubber tires. . .the list is endless.

Can't Spread Out?

Spread Up-In A Hammock!

One particularly intriguing method is found in the use of hammocks. Considerable space can be saved using this approach, for your garden can be stacked vertically! Two 4 x 4's, preferably of redwood, are needed at each end to provide the support. It is wise to bury the ends in concrete, for the weight will be considerable. Using a wire cable and chicken wire fencing, construct a sling between the supports. If the span is not too great, a center support will not be required. Lay a plastic sheet in the sling and perforate it to allow drainage. The number of tiers possible are determined by the depth of each. Fill with potting mixture and plant. We have found greatest success with carrots of the shorter variety, as opposed to those with longer roots. Also, most plants seem to do better when the whole arrangement lies in a North-South direction.

Watering is from above with the surplus water percolating down through the successive layers. So you see, with hammock gardening, not only is space saved, but water, also. This is a critical factor in many areas of the country.

We have briefly mentioned some of the favorite vegetables that can be adapted to container gardening.

Experimentation is always fun, but here is a list of some of those which have proven particularly successful:

ARTICHOKES - Globe	CUCUMBERS	ONIONS
BEANS - Both bush type	EGGPLANT	PEPPERS
and runner (Provide support)	ENDIVE	POTATOES
BEETS	FENNEL	RADISHES
CABBAGE	GARLIC	SQUASHES *
CARROTS	KALE	SWISS CHARD
CHILIS	LEEKS	TOMATOES †
CELERY	LETTUCE	

COLE VEGETABLES (Such as broccoli, Brussells sprouts, cauliflower, etc)

* Provide support for the vines, and slings made of discarded panty hose, tied to the trellis, can support the heavier squash as they develop.

† In some areas, determinate varieties are better suited. Check with your nursery for best varieties to plant in your area.

Fruits, too, can be grown in containers.

Many fruit trees come in dwarf varieties and produce full-size fruit. Some of the more frost-tender varieties will need to be brought indoors in the colder areas of the country.

APPLES	MELONS (see note regarding squash)		
CHERRIES	CITRUS	NECTARINES	PEACHES
PEARS	PLUMS	STRAWBERRIES	

(Strawberries are particularly beautiful draping over the sides of hanging pots or baskets. They also do well when planted in a "strawberry jar", a large clay pot with built-in planting pockets located all around the sides.)

Herbs

Herbs have long enjoyed a respected spot on the kitchen window sill. They flourish with a minimum of care and are readily available to lend their fresh goodness to many dishes. You can begin to snip the leaves as soon as the plant has a number of leaves. Use them as often as you need them, but if you are harvesting a lot, as for dehydrating, try not to remove more than one-third at a time.

(Some herbs tend to be invasive in a garden situation, so they actually do better when contained in pots.) The following is a list of some of the more common herbs:

BASIL	DILL	OREGANO	SAGE
CHERVIL	MARJORAM	PARSLEY	TARRAGON
CHIVES	MINT	ROSEMARY	THYME
CILANTRO (Coriander)			

So now you can see, no matter what your situation, you can enjoy the "fruits of your labors". Total self-sufficiency might not be possible for everyone but, to whatever degree, you can produce your own produce!

Putting Aside

This is a concept as old as nature itself. The oft-used example is that of the squirrel putting aside a supply of nuts. This behavior has even led to a popular expression, "squirreling it away", to describe saving for the future.

Until not too long ago, this was a common practice in our society. But how easy it has become over the years for us to run to the store to buy a can of this, or a package of that. Only now, are people beginning to realize what a toll this dependence has taken: Prices are spiraling out of sight, and closer looks at food labels are finding more additives than product!

Our forefathers managed to even out their food supply through the year, and they didn't have the benefit of the modern technology available to us today. Of course they didn't enjoy the abundance and variety we have become accustomed to, but today you can have the best of both worlds.

In ***A BITE OF INDEPENDENCE***, we discuss in great detail the various methods of storage: STORAGE OF FRESH FRUITS AND VEGETABLES; STORAGE OF DRY FOODS (such as beans and grains); DEHYDRATING, utilizing solar and conventional ovens, dehydrators, and microwave; PICKLING; CURING & SMOKING; CANNING; and FREEZING.

In this book we will tell you how to store your bulk grains, easy ways to dehydrate, and how to use that boon to modern day living: The freezer.

Storing Grains And Legumes

The treatment for storing dry material such as grains and beans is the same for all varieties. The material should be clean and of high quality. Wheat should be a hard, red, winter wheat with a protein content of at least 14% to 15%, and a moisture content of no more than 11%.

Corn can be obtained from a feed store at less cost. Just be certain to ask for FEED corn, NOT SEED corn. You do not want seed that has been treated with a fungicide which would, of course, be toxic.

Dry Ice

The easiest means of storage is with the use of poly buckets and dry ice. Using a 5 or a 6 gallon bucket, fill to within 3 inches from the top. Carefully, (for it can burn you hands), place a piece of dry ice, about 3 inches square and broken into chunks, on a small paper plate. Place this on the surface of the grain and loosely reposition the lid. Wait until a quick peek reveals the ice has evaporated, then hammer the lid firmly in place. The fumes created by the ice are carbon dioxide which is heavier than air. When they sink to the bottom of the bucket, they force the air out and create an inert atmosphere which discourages insects as long as the seal remains intact.

Nitrogen

The same principle applies to the use of Nitrogen. Although access to a nitrogen cylinder is harder to come by, it does the job speedily and well. Fill the container with the grain and insert the Nitrogen wand to the bottom. Position the lid so that it just allows room for the hand holding the wand. Move the wand up and down through the product to the count of 15 seconds for the 5 to 6 gallon size, or 2 to 3 seconds for the gallon size container. When the time has elapsed, quickly withdraw the wand and seal the can. With either of these two methods the grain can be stored indefinitely when kept in a cool, moisture free place.

Drying Fruits And Vegetables

One of the oldest means of food preservation, drying is still useful and convenient. Properly dried foods contain anywhere from 5% to 25% moisture and the reduction in volume greatly saves on storage.

Pretreating Vegetables: Pick only prime vegetables for drying and plan to dry them the same day, if possible. The flavor and color are better preserved if they are blanched after washing. This is accomplished by boiling or steaming: The latter, while taking longer, better preserves the nutrients.

To steam blanch, place a 2 inch layer of vegetables in a colander or wire basket on a rack above 2 inches of boiling water. (Four Chinese bamboo steamer baskets which stack together work well.) Cover the pot tightly and cook until the vegetables are heated through and wilted. A cross section should be translucent nearly to the center.

To boil blanch, use just enough water to cover the vegetables. Stir them in, gradually, once the water has come to a boil. Cover and cook as above, using the same water over for the same type of vegetable, replenishing as needed.

Pretreating Fuits: Use only fully-ripened fruits, ones that you would want to eat, since drying does nothing to improve the quality.

Unlike vegetables, blanching is not generally recommended for fruits. It gives them a cooked flavor and makes them soft and difficult to handle.

One way of pretreating fruits is to expose them to sulfur fumes. This method is described in ***A BITE OF INDEPENDENCE***. The alternative is to dip the cut fruit into lemon or orange juice and drain on paper towels.

Solar Drying

Solar drying can be unreliable unless the temperature is above 98° fahrenheit and the relative humidity is low. The vegetables or fruits are spread thinly on a non-galvanized screen or tray. Do not stack the trays. If the fruit is pitted, place the pitted side up.

To keep insects out, cover with cheesecloth or nylon netting, avoid touching the food. Turn over when the moisture in the pits evaporates. Turn the vegetables or fruits daily, and bring indoors if evening fog or dampness threatens. Fruits are dried until LEATHERY, while vegetables are dried until BRITTLE.

Oven Drying

Drying foods in the oven is possible, although it is not recommended for fruits that have been sulfured. The trays used should allow a clearance around all sides for the air to circulate. There needs to be at least 3 inches on top and 1½ inches around the sides. Place the trays no closer than 2 inches apart. Preheat the oven to 160°and either wipe the trays with oil, or spray lightly with non-stick spray. It is best to keep the load to a manageable amount of about 4 to 6 pounds at a time. Place a thermometer in the back of the top tray and prop the oven door open about 4 inches. Place a fan so the breeze will blow across the face of the opening and aid in the removal of the moisture. It is normal for the temperature to drop when the food is initially put in, but try to maintain the heat at 140°. Watch closely during the end, as this is when you find a tendency for the food to scorch. Turn the trays frequently to aid in even drying. Always let a sample cool thoroughly before testing for dryness.

Dehydrator Drying

A food dehydrator is the most reliable method of drying. One can be purchased for an amount that will fit nearly any budget, as they vary widely in cost and size and degree of sophistication. There are plans available for building your own and the plan for an effective yet simple homemade dehydrator can be found in ***A BITE OF INDEPENDENCE***.

As with oven dehydrating, trays need to be sprayed with a non-stick coating, or wiped lightly with oil. Arrange food, single layer deep, on the trays and place in the dehydrator which has been pre-heated to 160 °. A good thermometer, placed on the lowest tray, is advisable. The temperature will drop when the dehydrator is loaded. Bring it up to 140° and check the food every couple of hours. It takes less heat to maintain the temperature as completion nears, so watch closely to prevent scorching. Turn and rotate the trays. Drying can take from 4 to 16 hours, depending upon food being dried.

Packaging And Storing Dried Foods

When the fruits or vegetables are dry, (leathery for fruits, brittle for vegetables), put them in a non-metallic container to equalize the moisture content. With the exception of sulfured fruits, they should be Pasteurized to kill any spoilage organisms. To do this, place the food in glass jars and bake at 175° for 15 minutes, or at 150° for 30 minutes. Store them in either the glass jars, or in plastic bags, out of direct light.

Storage times vary with the product. Shelf life can be prolonged if the foods are kept in a cool, dark, dry place.

• Most vegetables can be kept for a year, with the exception of cabbage, carrots, and onions which will keep well for 6 months.

• Fruits, including tomatoes, and fruit leathers will generally keep 30 weeks at room temperature, 6 months in the refrigerator, and indefinitely, if frozen.

• Meats, including jerky, will keep 1 to 3 months if dried to the brittle stage, somewhat less if dried to the chewy stage. Any fat remaining in the meat will hasten the onset of rancidity, so trim carefully. One to three months seems to be the maximum when stored at room temperature. For longer storage, wrap tightly in plastic and freeze for up to 6 months.

Rehydrating Dried Foods

The water removed during drying needs to be replaced by soaking or cooking. Foods can either be covered with an equal amount of boiling water and allowed to steep for 5 minutes, or covered with cold water and allowed to soak for 1½ to 2 hours. Simmer until tender and liquid is absorbed. Rehydrated vegetables are best not used as side dishes, but rather as ingredients in casseroles, soups and sauces.

Tomatoes, greens and cabbages need no soaking, just cover them with water and simmer until tender. When added to chicken or beef broth, they form a hearty soup.

Pumpkin and squash strips need to be soaked overnight. Use them in place of fresh in your recipes.

Fruits to be used in baking can be softened by placing in a colander over boiling water and steamed until softened. As a snack, they can be softened by placing in a plastic bag with a few drops of water. Put in the refrigerator several hours until softened.

Hints And Tips For Using Your Dried Foods

1. Cut up leftover, or stale bread to make croutons, stuffing, or crumbs.
2. Dried celery leaves, leftover vegetables and onions, when combined with your favorite herbs and pulverized in the blender, become an instant soup mix.
3. Old, over-ripe bananas are occasionally found at the supermarket at greatly reduced prices, and when dried, make delicious sweet chips for snacking, or adding to homemade dry cereal.
4. Dried zucchini and cucumber slices make tasty chips to be served with yogurt or tofu dips.
5. Excess tomatoes can be dried and pulverized in the blender to be added to sauces and spaghetti to heighten the flavor.
6. Mushrooms are frequently a "loss leader" at the grocery, and when dried, they are an important ingredient in casseroles, omelettes, soups and sauces.
7. Dried, powdered berries are an excellent addition to punches and a novel topping to desserts.

Other Uses For The Food Dehyradtor

- To speed the rising of bread doughs
- To re-crisp stale crackers or cereals
- To dry flowers & herbs for sachets
- To dry homemade noodles and other pastas
- To make "leather" from over-ripe fruits, or from old, bottled fruits
- To dry granolas
- To incubate yogurt
- To dry citrus peels

Fruit & Tomato Leather

One of my children's favorite snacks is the fruit roll-up, found at an exorbitant price in the supermarket. It is merely fruit leather, created for mere pennies at home. In fact, one of my best leathers was made from apricots that were found to be woody and stringy after I canned them. They were recycled as leather, and since they were canned in a sugar syrup, needed no additional sweetening. Other old bottled fruits work well, also. Merely drain the syrup, puree in the blender, and pour 1/4 inch deep on a plastic lined jelly roll pan or cookie sheet that has a lip. Tip the tray so the entire surface is covered and place in the sun, covered with netting to exclude insects, for two to three days. Or, you may dry it in the oven, set at the lowest setting with the door cracked open, for 4 to 5 hours. If you have a dehydrator, it will take 4 to 5 hours at 140°.

The same procedure is used for fresh fruits, including tomatoes. Be sure they are ripe, to over-ripe. With tomatoes use no sugar; with other fruits, your own preference will determine what you use. If a sweeter leather is desired, add 2 Tablespoons either sugar, corn syrup, or honey per quart of puree.

When properly dried, leather will be sticky to the touch, but an edge can be lifted and peeled back from the plastic. When it reaches this stage, simply roll it up in one piece, plastic and all, to be peeled as it is eaten.

Fruit leather is good as is, or it can be made into a beverage by adding 5 parts of water and blending it in the blender. It can also be used in cooking, and pie fillings, and a topping for desserts.

Beef Jerky

Another expensive snack item easily made at home, is beef jerky. Choose very lean meat, such as flank steak, or any other lean meat, and cut it into strips about 4 to 12 inches long, by 1/4 to 1/2 inches thick and 1 to $1^1/_2$ inches wide. It will help to partially freeze the meat before cutting it. Trim off all visible fat. To make about 1 pound jerky, you will need:

4 pounds lean beef
3 Tablespoons vinegar
2 Tablespoons lemon juice
1 teaspoon seasoned salt
1/3 Cup soy sauce
2 Tablespoons sugar
1 teaspoon onion powder
1/4 teaspoon garlic powder
Few drops liquid smoke, if desired

Marinate the meat in the mixture overnight in the refrigerator. Remove from the marinade and pat dry with paper towels. To sun dry: It helps to use an open barbecue, if you have one. Line the bowl with foil to reflect the heat. Lay the strips of meat over the rack; they may touch, but do not overlap. Place in the direct sun, and depending upon the temperature, it should take about 4 to 6 days to complete drying. Bring indoors at nighttime, or when weather threatens. To oven dry: Drape the strips over the oven rack as for the sun drying method. Line the bottom of the oven with foil to catch any drips. Set the temperature to 140° and prop the door open. The use of a fan will help remove the moisture-laden air. Full drying should take about 11 hours. Take care you do not cook the meat, just keep the oven warm.

Drying Herbs In The Microwave

To dry fresh herbs in the microwave oven, gather them early in the morning. Rinse them well and pat dry with paper towels. Remove the thicker, woody stems and spread in a single layer on paper towel on a microwaveable plate. Heat on high power, testing frequently until dry and brittle. Times will vary with individual ovens. When crisp, cool and store in airtight, labeled jars. Remember, when using dried herbs, the flavor is intensified, so use a little less than you would with fresh.

Freezing

Undoubtedly, freezing is the easiest method of preserving food. Frozen foods retain their color, fresh flavor and nutritive value far better than those preserved by any other method. Used efficiently, a home freezer can round out your whole home storage plan, in addition to allowing better use of valuable time.

To illustrate this point, for a short time Jan Woolley's garden produced at a rate faster than she could handle. At this writing she had 50 pounds of frozen, whole tomatoes in plastic bags awaiting the day she could thaw them and prepare a delicious tomato sauce to be bottled.

With the exception of a freezer, there is little investment in equipment needed. Everything you need for processing food for freezing can be found in the kitchen, and containers can be varied and may come from many sources.

The following is a list that might be helpful.

MATERIAL	SUGGESTED USE
Aluminum foil	poultry, meat, fish, asparagus, corn on the cob any food
Foil containers	to be reheated or baked in conventional oven; cover with foil and seal
Freezer paper	meat, fish, poultry, baked goods, corn on the cob (shiny side toward food)
Thin plastic wrap	meat, fish, baked goods, corn on the cob; easily and firmly molds to food, does not become brittle
Plastic bags	vegetables, fruits, (dry packed), cookies, baked foods, sandwiches; gently squeeze to exclude air
Plastic cartons (with tight-fitting lids)	vegetables, sugared fruits, made up dishes, casseroles; allow space for expansion - easy to stack, reusable
Tin cans with lids (coffee or shortening)	cookies, candies, nuts; separate layers of cookies, etc. with waxed paper
Canning jars	soups, sauces, made up dishes, vegetables, sugared fruits;do not worry about sealing jars,just allowspace for expansion and put lids on.

Some of the economic advantages of a freezer are being able to buy foods fresh and in season when the price is favorable. Grocery stores frequently offer items at a discount to lure customers in to their stores. Even small gardens can be quite productive... All these situations coupled with a freezer add up to quite a savings on the food bill.

Keep in mind when preparing food for the freezer to be sure to use only top quality. Food will come out no better than it was when it went in. Freezing does not improve quality, but with a few simple hints, you can be assured of high quality meals from you freezer.

- Plan the freezer load. Don't take up space with things readily available all year long.

- Freeze what you anticipate your family's needs will be until the food is available the following season. Don't load up on one food to the exclusion of all else.
- Freeze in sizes convenient for your family. Smaller sizes freeze and thaw more quickly.
- Freeze at prime picking time and work rapidly. Try to freeze vegetables within 2 hours after they are picked.
- Date packages and rotate inventory.
- Refreeze thawed foods only if ice crystals remain in the center.
- Seal carefully to keep air out. Air robs quality.
- A freezer works harder to freeze something than it does to maintain a frozen state. Don't freeze more than 3 pounds per cubic foot in a 24 hour period.
- A freezer works most economically when it is 3/4 full. Don't cram food in so tightly that air cannot circulate, nor so loosely that cold air is wasted.
- Try to organize your freezer into long term storage compartments for meats, vegetables, fruits, etc. and shorter term items such as baked goods, sausages, lunchmeats, prepared foods, etc.

The following list should provide some guidelines as to storage times. Remember, that food doesn't automatically go bad when the date expires, it simply starts losing quality.

Meat

Beef	**Months**
steaks-roasts	12
franks	3
hamburger	3
organ meats	4
Lamb	
roasts	9
Pork	
cured	4
fresh	6-8
sausages	4-6
Most game	12
Stews & soups	3
Cooked meat dishes	3

Poultry

Chicken	**Months**
Cut up	9
whole	12
cut up	6
livers	3
Turkey	
whole	12
Cooked poultry	6
sliced with gravy	6
meat pies	6
fried chicken	4
Duck, whole	6
Goose, whole	6

Seafood

Raw Fish	Months		Months
lean fish	9	shellfish	4
fatty fish	4	crabs/lobsters	2
salmon	3	shrimp	4
Cooked fish	**Months**		
pies-creoles, etc.	3		

Vegetables	Months
Whole kernel corn, mashed pumpkin	16
Lima beans, broccoli, Brussels sprouts, cauliflower, carrots, greens, okra, all peas, winter squash, sweet potatoes, turnips, all beans, corn on the cob, cream style corn, eggplant, kohlrabi, mixed vegetables	
peppers, summer squash	12
Asparagus, mushrooms	8
Potatoes, stuffed/French fried	3

Fruits	Months
apples, apricots, cherries, cranberries, peaches, pineapples, raspberries, rhubarb, strawberries	16
blueberries, currants, coconut, dates, figs, gooseberries, grapes, juices, melons, oranges, grapefruit, plums, prunes	12
mixed fruits, pears	8

Dairy	Months	Baked Goods	Months
butter	6	white bread	3
cream	4	wheat bread	8
milk	6	rolls, baked	8
cottage cheese	3	rolls, brown & serve	6
cheese	5	rolls, unbaked	1
eggs	12		
Cakes			
baked	4	Baked pies	2
baked, frosted	3	Unbaked pies	4
unbaked	1	Baked quick breads	3
cupcakes	3	Cooked Leftovers	1
baked cookies	12	Sandwiches	1
doughnuts	3	Danish pastries	3

Some things do not freeze well. These include: Custards, cream fillings, meringue based icings, fried foods, (with the exception of French fries and Onion rings), mayonnaise, gelatin, and cooked egg whites.

Freezing Vegetables

With the exception of green peppers, onions, and tomatoes, all vegetables should be blanched before freezing.

Blanching entails scalding the vegetable to arrest the action of certain enzymes. These enzymes are responsible for the loss of flavor, color, and vitamins which would occur during the freezing process if blanching didn't take place.

There are five basic steps to freezing vegetables

1. **Blanching**: This is done by bringing 1 gallon of water to a boil in a large pot.
2. **Immersing:** Place no more than 1 pound of washed, trimmed, cut up vegetables in the boiling water.
3. **Covering & Timing:** See chart, as time varies with each vegetable.
4. **Chilling:** When time is up, **chill** quickly by rinsing in cold or ice water. The chilling time should equal the scalding time.
5. **Packing:** Pack into chosen containers, label, and freeze.

VEGETABLE	TIPS	TIME IN MINUTES
Artichoke, Globe	Cut tips off, wash in cold water	7
Artichoke, Jerusalem	Wash peel or scrape	3-5
Asparagus	depending upon size	$1^1/_2$-3
Beans, lima	depending upon size	1-3
Beans, snap (green)		3
Beans, soy	Boil green pods Cool, squeeze beans out, rinse and drain	5
Beets	Cut tops off, wash Cool, peel, cut up, if desired	cook until tender
Broccoli	Soak in brine 30 minutes to remove insects. (1 cup salt per 1 gallon water) Rinse, drain	3-4
Brussels Sprouts	depending upon size	3-5
Cabbage	Cut into wedges or coarse shreds	3 wedges $1^1/_2$ shredded

VEGETABLE	TIPS	TIME IN MINUTES
Carrots	Large quantities can be put through the rinse cycle of your automatic clothes washer for ease in preparing!	3 cut-up, 5 whole
Cauliflower	See Broccoli	3-4
Corn	depending on size	8-10
Eggplant	Peel, slice 1/3 inch thick. Add 5 teaspoons citric acid, or 1/2 cup lemon juice to blanching water	4
Greens	Avoid matting the leaves	2
Kohlrabi	Peel bark, slice centers. Leave small roots whole	2-slices, 3 whole
Mushrooms	Add 3 tsp lemon juice, or 1/2 teaspoon ascorbic acid per quart of blanching water	4-whole small 3-large sliced
Okra	depending upon size	3-5
Onions	Peel as for eating	3-7 until heated through
Onions, green	wash and mince	Do not blanch
Parsnips		3
Peas, all kinds	Remove tips and strings from snow peas	2
Peppers	Freeze halves, chopped, strips, or whole	Do not blanch
Potatoes, Irish	Peel or scrape	3-5
Pumpkins	Peel, deseed, steam or bake until soft. Mash	
Squash, summer		3
Squash, winter	Bake at 375° cut side down until tender. Mash	
Tomatoes, Whole	Wash, dry and freeze on trays. When hard, put in plastic bags. To thaw, put in cup of water and microwave on high until skin slips. They do not slice well, but can be chopped and added to salads and tacos, etc. for fresh taste.	Do Not blanch
Tomatoes, cooked	Wash, core, cut and cook. Put through a food mill. To concentrate, boil until volume reduced by half.	
Turnips		3

Freezing Fruits

Freezing fruits is much more simple a project than the freezing of vegetables. Begin with top quality, ripe fruit. Wash it well and cut up, if needed. The quickest and easiest method is to simply place in plastic bags and put in the freezer.

Sugaring, if desired, is accomplished by putting the fruit in a large bowl and adding sugar, to taste. Wait a few minutes for syrup to form from the juices, then package into chosen containers.

Some prefer to freeze fruits with an added sugar syrup. To do this, make a syrup using 2 Cups sugar to 4 Cups water. Heat until sugar is dissolved and chill before using. Prepare fruit, put in containers, (jars or plastic cartons work best) pour the syrup over, leaving 1 inch headspace for expansion, and seal. Grapes freeze well in this manner.

Freezing Meats

The important thing to remember when freezing meats is to make the package as airtight as possible. The clear packaging from the supermarket is generally not appropriate for long term freezing. Meat should be rewrapped snugly in freezer paper before being placed in the freezer.

For best quality, thaw in the refrigerator for 12 to 24 hours. If in a hurry, meat can be thawed under cold running water.

Don't overlook the fact that meat doesn't have to be completely thawed before cooking. More juices are retained and less flavor lost when meat is in at least a partially frozen state. Simply start it at a little lower temperature than you would normally use and cook it for 10 to 15 minutes longer per pound.

Fish Farming

This is a subject that always arouses considerable interest when mentioned. You can raise - in your very own back yard - delicious fresh fish! Surprisingly, it isn't difficult to do nor is it expensive. It is having an aquarium on a grand scale: any large container can serve. Some use children's wading pools; in fact a tank 12 feet in diameter and just 2 feet deep can raise up to 100 pounds of fish in one growing season of 5 to 6 months.

The success of your harvest is dependent upon three factors: **WATER QUALITY**, **OXYGEN CONTENT**, and **TEMPERATURE**.

Water Quality

Water Quality is rated by the degree of acidity or alkalinity it possesses on the pH scale. Testing strips are available at aquarium stores and even some garden nurseries. Alkaline conditions are represented by the higher numbers on the scale and acid by the lower. With the scale running from 1 through 14, 7 is considered neutral. Fish seem to do best if the water is kept on the slightly acid side, the ideal being around 6.5 to 7. To adjust your water, add gypsum to reduce alkalinity, lime to reduce the acidity.

Check your water for heavy metals, as they are toxic to fish. Iron, lead, and copper in concentrations as low as three parts per million can affect them. A water supply that is chlorinated must be filtered through charcoal before use.

Oxygen

Oxygen helps the fish to be healthier and grow faster. In fact, an aerator can double the harvest. A pump that sprays the water through the air is one means of aeration. Another is to locate the filter - containing charcoal and crushed lava rock, sea shells, or sand - above the tank. The water is pumped up through the filter and allowed to free fall back to the tank below. This method has two advantages: the water is oxygenated by its passage through the air, and it picks up naturally-occuring bacteria from the filter. The action of these bacteria occurs within the tank serving to render the fish waste harmless.

Temperature

The temperature, in large part, determines the type of fish you can raise successfully. It varies with different species of fish. Trout are cold water fish and thrive in a temperature of 54° to 56°. They can even survive to near freezing. Tilapia, on the other hand, are a tropical fish related to bass. They do better in a temperature of 80° to 90°, making them ideal to raise in the summer.

Two weeks prior to acquiring the fish, set up the tank, checking to assure the filter and aeration system work properly. It is helpful, if possible, to obtain a couple of gallons of water from someone with an aquarium as this will speed up the establishment of the helpful bacteria.

Begin with about 1 pound of fingerlings for every cubic foot of water. They should arrive in plastic bags of water. Place these fish, bags and all, in the water to float while the temperature equalizes. This should take approximately one hour and helps avoid thermal shock during the transition.

Fish Feed Garden - Garden Feeds Fish

Thriving on a diet of algae, occasional grass clippings, a pinch of chicken manure, your fish should reach eating size of 1/2 to 1 pound in around 5 to 6 months. They can also be fed a diet of soy flour, grain meal, midge larvae, chopped earthworms, or commercial feed. Take care not to over-feed. If you find feed left over, reduce, or even skip the next day's feeding. When the system is operating well, a cycle is established: water, rich in nitrogenous fish waste is put on the garden, and garden scraps are fed to the fish. Although artificially created, it is an ecosystem that is refreshing to observe.

More on Tilapia

With most of our experience dealing with Tilapia, here are a few observations that might be of interest: There are over a dozen species of Tilapia, ranging in color from dark brown to black.

Plastic vessels, covered with holes to admit the fish and placed on the bottom of the tank, offer shelter and encourage them to breed rapidly. You can expect to find new young (fry) about every 30 days.

As a rule, Tilapia take very good care of their young, but the very small fry sometimes find themselves becoming the main course. If this should happen, separate them by suspending a bag, made from muslin or netting formed around a wire frame, in the water and placing the fry within.

Tilapia exhibit good disease resistance, rapid growth, and a good degree of fertility; all qualities that make them a very profitable, low maintenance source of protein. And all this is possible with the confines of your own back yard.

For further information, contact fisheries, your local library, or the Game and Fish Department in your area. **Good fishing!**

Home Butchering

One of the advantages of this program is the flexibility that is built into the diet. While vegetarians enjoy those parts that relate to them, meat lovers are also able to find their wants satisfied.

One of the authors (Jan), lives on an acre where she raises and butchers all the meats her family uses. Her family enjoys tasty beef, lamb, pork, chicken, turkey and rabbit throughout the year, and roast goose at Christmas. This is eaten with peace of mind, knowing that their home-produced meats are free from growth hormones, antibiotics, or pesticide residues.

A ***BITE OF INDEPENDENCE*** goes into great detail on the actual butchering of the various meats, but for the sake of this book, we need to reduce our scope somewhat.

Rabbit

While we realize that not everyone has the room to raise a steer, or other large livestock, practically anyone can find room (even in a basement or garage), to raise a few rabbits. Once you can get yourself past the Easter Bunny - Peter Rabbit stage, you will find that the meat is delightful. Tasting very similar to chicken, and prepared much the same way, you will find that rabbit is very economical to raise. The ratio of feed to weight gain is quite advantageous and rabbits grow rapidly. This is desirable for they are butchered at an early age, generally between 12 to 24 weeks of age.

Home Butchering Is More Humane

Begin with isolating the animal in a calm, quiet environment for 24 hours. During this time, withhold all feed, yet allow unlimited access to fresh water. This treatment results in a carcass much easier to clean, and the calm treatment produces a better quality meat than would be obtained from an excited, agitated animal.

Although the experts can kill them by quickly breaking the neck, I find that I am less traumatized by shooting at point blank with a .22. Immediately after the kill, sever the head with a hatchet or sharp knife and hang by the hind feet to permit a thorough bleeding. This rapid bleeding improves the quality and keeping properties of the meat.

Next, cut off the tail and front feet. Cut the skin around each hind foot, then slit the skin on the inside of each hind leg from that cut down to the crotch.

This results in one continuous incision from foot to foot. Then simply peel the skin off, beginning with the top. (Since the rabbit is hanging, this means you will begin with the hind legs.) It will be like taking a glove off, inside out. Loosen around the anus with the knife and remove the skin in one piece. The skin can be discarded, or slit, salted and tanned later.

The skinned rabbit is then rinsed well in cool water to remove blood and debris. Carefully slit the abdominal wall from the breastbone up to the anus. Take care that you don't puncture the bladder or the intestine and foul the meat. Cut around the anus and insert your hand through the abdominal incision, pulling the anus and attached intestines out through the incision. Pull everything else out and carefully cut the gall bladder, (the little sac of green bile), free from the liver. Discard it and wash the liver and heart. Organ meats do not keep well, so refrigerate immediately.

Rinse the carcass well in cold running water and pat dry with paper towels. Place the whole rabbit in a plastic bag and age in the refrigerator for 3 to 4 days to tenderize and improve the flavor. After aging, cut up and prepare as desired.

How Can I Fix Rabbit?

Rabbit meat is a little drier than chicken, but it can be used interchangeably in any chicken recipe and it is delicious roasted or barbecued whole. Rabbit meat may also be canned or frozen for later enjoyment.

Butchering Without Killing

For those of you who can't get past the thought of killing your own meat there are still ways to save money on most meat purchases.

Occasionally, the meat department in the supermarket will have a special on some of the larger cuts of meat. Sometimes you can even find large boneless cuts, trimmed and packaged in plastic.

Before deciding that these cuts are too large for your family, or thinking strictly in terms of company meals, stop and reconsider. By taking them home and doing a little cutting yourself, you can frequently end up with 3 or 4 varied meals from just one primal cut.

A large top round roast of beef, for example, can be cut into two smaller roasts, several steaks, and meat for cubing, or grinding. So you can enjoy pot roasts with vegetables, Swiss steaks with onions, stews, Hungarian goulash, Salisbury steak with mushroom gravy, meat loaf, or Swedish meatballs on rice.

Likewise, boneless beef tip can be cut into steaks for pan-frying or braising, roasts, and cubes or ground beef. From this cut, then, you can enjoy tender roast sirloin, beef burgundy, stew, or any number of ground beef recipes.

Sometimes in the spring, a good buy can be found on a leg of lamb. Taken home and cut up, it can become roast leg of lamb studded with cloves of garlic, tender lamb steaks, and the shank can be cubed for use in shish kabob, or lamb curry.

Fresh pork shoulder can yield a good roast, pork steaks, and cubes for pork stew with cabbage, or stir-fry.

So you can see that by buying with forethought, you can fill your freezer with cuts you might not have thought you could afford. A great savings can be realized just by your being your own butcher.

If you would like to learn more ways to save money on your meat purchases, there is an excellent book available on the subject. Written by Vince Scalise, a third-generation butcher and professional meat retailer, ***MEAT SENSE*** is full of inside tips designed to give the customer the advantage. More than a guide to deceptive retailing practices, its humorous approach to more informed meat purchasing makes for an entertaining read. It is available by calling, toll-free, 1 (800) 688-3491, or you can write to: 124 South Isabel Street, Glendale, California, 91205.

Skinning A Rabbit

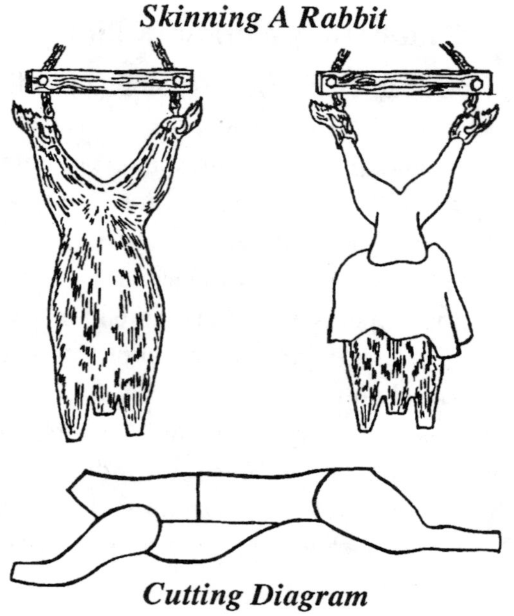

Cutting Diagram

Cheese and Yogurt

There are few things that bring more satisfaction than cutting into a wheel of beautiful cheese and knowing that you made it yourself. For your own peace of mind, you know that it is additive-free, having in it only what you have put in. Homemade cheeses make unbeatable gifts: original, inexpensive, and always welcome.

Makes Sense and Saves Cents

Cheese is economical to make, too, if you exclude your labor. You will need to make an initial investment in a good dairy or yogurt thermometer as well as rennet, and cheese culture. However, when you amortize this cost over several batches of cheese, the price becomes minor, indeed. The main cost will be for the milk. Figure a yield of approximately 1 pound of cheese for each gallon of milk used, and you can see that making your own cheese makes sense as well as saving cents.

The basis for any cheese is, of course, milk. You can use cow's or goat's milk, whole milk, skim milk, raw milk, or even reconstituted powdered milk.

Why Raw Milk Is Preferred

The best cheeses are made of whole raw milk and are safe to eat when aged for a least 60 days. If you know that the cow is healthy, not suffering from mastitis or receiving antibiotics, and if you practice good hygiene, the cheese will be safe, even if eaten fresh.

Raw milk is most desirable because it contains natural bacteria which impart much of the flavor and character to the cheese. Skim milk makes a harder, drier, more compact cheese, one more suited to grating than table use. However, if you are trying to reduce your fat intake, a fairly acceptable cheese can be made using half whole milk, and half 2% milk.

But yes, You Can Use Store bought

If using plain homogenized milk, you will have to exercise some care since the curds are more delicate than those formed from raw milk. It helps to heat this milk a couple of degrees higher than the recipe calls for, and to cook it awhile longer, however, with a little practice, a surprisingly good cheese can be made. We would hesitate to recommend this procedure for a beginner, though. It is difficult to do without knowing beforehand what the various steps should look like. Fortunately, for those dependent upon store milk, there is calcium chloride. It is found at some pharmacies, or can be ordered from cheese making supply houses.(See the list at end of this chapter) One quarter teaspoon added to every two gallons of homogenized milk helps the curd form in a manner similar to that of raw milk.

One more word about milk here. Cows provide a larger quantity of milk and make cream more readily available for butter making. However, for economy, not much can beat a goat. Goat's milk cheeses are delicious and much prized. The procedures are similar to cow's milk cheeses with one exception. The curds are very fragile and require gentle handling. Heat the milk 2 or 3 degrees LOWER than the recipe calls for.

Whatever type of milk you use, be sure that it is of the highest quality and as fresh as possible.

With Or Without A Starter

It is possible to make cheese without a starter if raw milk is used. Due to the natural bacteria found in the milk, clabbering can take place when the milk is allowed to stand at room temperature for 12 to 24 hours. When ready to begin making the cheese, simply use half clabbered and half fresh morning milk.

Generally, however, a starter is used and it can be either commercial powdered starter, or buttermilk or yogurt. It is essential if using buttermilk or yogurt that you purchase the very freshest and do not open it until ready to begin.

Buttermilk is used for cheeses such as the colbys and cheddars, while yogurt makes the Italian type cheeses such as Mozzarella and Parmesan. Yogurt also is used in making your own homemade yogurt. Check the carton first to be sure that it contains active culture. If it doesn't contain live bacteria it will be of no use to you.

Rennet is an enzyme used in some cheeses to aid in the coagulation. Be sure to get cheese making rennet, not Junket rennet. It may be found in some pharmacies or health food stores, or may be ordered from cheese making supply houses.

Coloring your cheeses is an option. While it doesn't affect the flavor of a cheese, it does lend eye appeal to those accustomed to a yellow cheese. Standard food coloring is not satisfactory, as it tends to wash out with the whey. A special, nontoxic coloring, made from the seed of a tropical plant - the annato - is used in cheese making. It, too, can be purchased from cheese making supply houses.

Minimal Materials Are Needed

At least two pots are needed, one to fit inside the other in a double-boiler arrangement. Stainless steel is preferred wherever there is contact with milk, however plastic or enamel ware can be used. Aluminum or cast iron should **NOT** be used as there would be a reaction set up between the metal and the acids produced by the cheese.

You will need a thermometer with a range between 20° F to 220° F. I find a floating dairy thermometer convenient, however yogurt or even wine making thermometers work well.

A sharp knife with a blade long enough to reach the bottom of the pot and a stainless steel stirring spoon or flattened ladle, each with a long handle, are also necessary. These are needed for cutting and stirring the curds.

Cheesecloth or any porous fabric, such as muslin, is needed for draining and pressing the curds. Two square yards should be enough, but it is always nice to have extra on hand when some cheeses need to be redressed several times. It can be washed and re-used repeatedly.

Cheese molds and presses are as varied as the imagination. Just bear in mind the principle of containment and pressure. Any container, such as a large can punched all over with holes (from the inside, out), or a round plastic jar with the top and bottom removed - punched with holes - will do. The holes are needed to allow the whey to escape when pressure is applied.

Cut to fit the inside diameter of the can or jar is the follower, or plunger. It can be cut from a small board and it is upon the follower that the pressure is exerted. Place a small brick on end on top of the follower which is, in turn, resting on the cheesecloth wrapped curds. Place a heavy weight such as a gallon jug of water on top of it all, and you have an elementary press. See the end of this chapter for more ideas on making cheese presses.

Cleanliness Determines Quality

One word of caution before you begin your cheese making: Quality begins and ends with cleanliness. Keep everything that comes in contact with the milk scrupulously clean. Cheese depends upon the action of bacteria and you do not want to introduce any undesirable ones. Thoroughly wash all the utensils before you begin and wash them again after use. When washing anything that comes in contact with milk, rinse in cool water first. This preliminary step prevents the milk from "cooking" on the surface when the utensil is next washed in hot, soapy water. Rinse well, and scald with boiling water. Plastic and wooden utensils cannot be scalded, but are sanitized by rinsing with a chlorine bleach solution (2 Tablespoons bleach to 1 gallon of water). Be sure to rinse well so no trace of bleach remains.

We are limited in this volume to the most frequently used cheeses: Colby (used as a mild longhorn-type cheese in most of our recipes), cottage cheese, and yogurt.

Cottage Cheese

While we give the recipe for one gallon, you may find it more convenient to make it up in three gallon batches.

1 Gallon skimmed or reconstituted powdered milk
10 Ounces cultured Mesophilic starter (commercial),
OR
1/2 Cup fresh buttermilk
1-3 teaspoons salt
Cream or half-and-half

In a large pot over hot water, heat the milk to 88°. Remove from the heat. Add the buttermilk or starter and stir periodically for 30 minutes. Cover with the lid and place the pot in a warm place where it can set, undisturbed, until a curd is formed. This can take anywhere from overnight, to one and a half days. It will be a soft jell, covered with watery whey when it is ready for the next step.

With the curd knife, make vertical slices, 1/2 inch apart. Turn the pot around and repeat the process, perpendicular to the first cuts. Next, make diagonal cuts at a 45° angle, 1/2 inch apart. Repeat from the other side, and you should then have a pot full of roughly 1/2 inch cubes floating in the whey.

Allow the curds to rest for 30 minutes. Add about 2 quarts of hot tap water, stirring gently. Over hot water, begin cooking the cheese, stirring once in awhile to keep the curds from matting.

It will take up to 90 minutes or more for the curds to reach the desired firmness. As they cook, they shrink in size. When the desired firmness is reached, pour off the water/whey mixture using a sieve to trap any errant curds. Stop when the curds are barely covered then add cold tap water. Pour off and repeat with fresh cold water.

When the curds are sufficiently chilled, pour into a cheesecloth-lined colander and allow to drain for 30 minutes. Break the mass up in a large bowl and add salt to taste. For Farmer's cheese, press lightly in a cheese press. For creamed cottage cheese, stir in cream or half and half to taste. (This cheese absorbs quite a bit of cream. The next day you may wish to add more cream or milk to adjust the consistency.)

Suggestions For Use

- Mix with shredded Colby or cheddar for a cheese enchilada filling.
- Mix in chopped chives, crushed pineapple and/or maraschino cherries.
- To fill blintzes or crepes: process in a blender and add a beaten egg, sugar to taste, and a little orange juice concentrate.
- Use in place of ricotta cheese when making lasagna.

Colby (Longhorn-Type) Cheese

This is often thought of as a mild form of cheddar. It has a higher moisture content than that of cheddar and therefore, doesn't keep as long. That disadvantage is offset by the fact that it is ready to eat sooner. This is the cheese I make most often, due to its versatility, ease in making, and relatively short aging time. My family goes through a lot of it.

2 Gallons whole milk **2 Tablespoons salt**
1 Cup fresh buttermilk OR **2 Ozs Mesophilic starter** (commercial)
1/8 tablet cheese color (optional)**, dissolved in 1/4 Cup cool water**

Over hot water heat the milk to 86°. Add the buttermilk or starter, stir and let ripen, off the heat, for 1/2 to 1 hour. The container of warm water should be sufficient to maintain the temperature at 86°. Keep covered. If a yellow cheese is desired, add the diluted coloring.

With the temperature at 86°, add the diluted rennet by pouring it over the ladle into the milk. Stir with an up-and-down motion for one minute. (If using non-homogenized milk, stir the surface in a circular motion for a minute to prevent the cream from rising.) Cover and let stand, undisturbed, for 30 to 40 minutes while the curd develops. Test if ready by inserting a clean finger into the curd at a 45° angle. Bring it straight up and if the curd breaks cleanly over the finger, it is ready. Using the long curd knife, cut into 1/2 inch cubes. (See directions for cottage cheese). Let it rest for 5 minutes. Then over hot water, begin the cooking. Cook, stirring gently, for approximately 35 minutes, or until it reaches 102°. You should do this slowly, no more than 2° every 5 minutes.

Treat the curd very gently, you do not want to bleed any of the butterfat into the whey which should be the color of greenish lemonade. Remove from the heat and allow it to rest for 20 to 30 minutes while the curds firm up. Stir them occasionally to keep them from matting. At this stage, they should resemble popped corn. Pour off the whey and drain the curds for a few minutes in a colander. Return them to the pot and gently break them up with the fingers. With the fingers, work in the salt.

Scoop the curds into a mold which has been lined with a damp cheesecloth. Cover with another small piece of cheesecloth and position the follower on the top. Place in the press and press lightly for 10 to 20 minutes. Flip the cheese over and repeat. Do this several times during the next two hours, increasing the pressure each time. Finally, remove the cheese from the press and rewrap it in a fresh, dampened cheesecloth. Return it to the press where it will remain for 12 hours. Take it from the press, peel off the cheesecloth and trim the ragged edges with a sharp knife. Place on a rack or reed mat and allow the cheese to air dry for 3 to 4 days to form a rind. This is best done at room temperature, unless beads of butterfat sweat onto the surface. In that case, it is too warm and should air dry in the refrigerator. Turn the cheese over several times daily and when dry to the touch, dip in cheese wax which has been liquified over hot water. (Cheese wax is available at cheese supply houses.) Or if you prefer, you may coat the cheese with butter instead of wax. Butter with fresh butter daily for 2 weeks, then two or three times a week for the remainder of the aging period.

Age the cheese in a temperature of approximately 50 degrees to 55 degrees, with a humidity of 85%. A vegetable drawer in the refrigerator generally satisfies this requirement. Turn the cheese over daily for the first week, then several times weekly thereafter to prevent moisture from collecting on the bottom. The cheese can be eaten after 1½ months, the flavor intensifying with time. Six months is considered ideal for full flavor development, although I seldom wait that long.

This recipe yields about 2 pounds of cheese.

Suggestions For Use

- Use as you would any longhorn cheese. (Longhorn is simply a shape, not a kind of cheese.)
- Good in Mexican cooking, frequently used in connection with Monterey Jack cheese.
- Stir shredded Colby into a basic white sauce, add a dash of Worcestershire sauce, and you have a good cheese sauce for vegetables, Welsh Rarebit, etc.
- Mix shredded Colby into biscuit dough, topping the baked biscuits with poached or scrambled eggs.
- Crumble on top of cooked, drained broccoli in the pan, cover with a lid and serve when the cheese has melted.
- Crumble on top of mixed green salads.
- Use for grilled cheese sandwiches.

Yogurt

While not generally thought of as a cheese, making yogurt uses many of the same techniques, and the results are wonderful. Almost everybody loves yogurt. What more healthful snack can you have in the refrigerator when your children come running in from school, than a cup of fresh homemade yogurt? Even the expensive, fruited ones that children clamor for are simple to make and keep on hand.

Doctors will frequently advise their patients who have been on extended antibiotic treatment to eat yogurt in order to re-establish the beneficial organisms depleted by the antibiotics.

Yogurt requires a warm, undisturbed place in which to incubate. Although a yogurt maker is nice to have, it certainly isn't essential. In fact, if your family really likes yogurt, you'll find that the yogurt makers do not make enough.

Of the many methods of incubation discussed in ***A Bite Of Independence***, the easiest is found in the use of your oven. Simply pour the yogurt mixture in a covered casserole dish and place in an oven which has been preheated to 100°. Turn off the heat and close the door where it will remain overnight. The next morning, add fruit, if desired, and refrigerate. It will thicken up as it chills.

Basic Yogurt

This recipe contains powdered milk which isn't essential to the making of yogurt. The increased milk solids provided by the powdered milk do, however, enrich its food value and help assure a firmer, less watery product. This produces a yogurt more similar in texture to the commercial brands.

2 Cups whole milk
1 1/3 Cups instant nonfat dry milk
1 3/4 Cups warm water
1/4 Cup fresh, plain yogurt for starter
(be sure it contains **active** culture)

Mix the milk with the powdered milk. Heat the mixture in the top of a double boiler until it reaches 180°. Do not boil. Cool to about 100° and discard the skin that may have formed.

Blend the yogurt starter with the warm water and add to the milk. Mix well and pour into the container you have chosen. Incubate for 3 1/2 hours up to overnight.* Cover and refrigerate. It will thicken as it chills.

* Reserve 1/4 Cup for your next batch starter. Repeat, each batch until it grows too weak to do the job. Then start over with more store-bought.

Sweetened Vanilla Yogurt

Add 1/4 Cup either white or brown sugar to the milk before scalding. Adds 2 teaspoons vanilla at the same time you add the starter. Proceed as with the basic yogurt recipe.

Fruited Yogurt

Fruited yogurts are easy to make and the variations are many. The basic procedure remains the same. The amount of yogurt to use is one recipe's worth of either the basic, or sweetened vanilla yogurt. To the completed yogurt add **$1\frac{1}{2}$ Cups sweetened fruit** and 1/2 **Cup of prepared juice.**

(To prepare the juice, heat with 1 envelope of unflavored gelatin, stirring until the gelatin is completely dissolved.)

Mix well and chill 2 to 3 hours before eating.

Supply Sources

New England Cheesemaking Supply Co.
P. O. Box 85
Ashfield, MA 01330
(413)628-3808

Daisyfresh Dairy Cultures
Box 36-S
Santa Cruz, CA 95063

Chr. Hansen's Laboratory Outlet 9015 W. Maple St.
Milwaukee, WI 53214-4298
(414) 476-3630

The Cheesemaking Supply
260 Moore Rd.
Butler, PA 16001
(412) 282-0026

Caprine Supply *
P. O. Box Y, 3301 W. 83rd St.
DeSoto, KS 66018
(913) 585-1191
* Specializes in goat supplies, but many items apply to cows.

Elementary Cheese Press

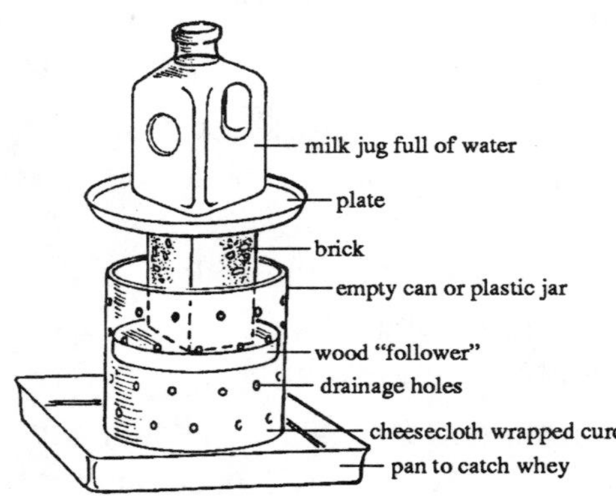

Press Made From Trailer Jack

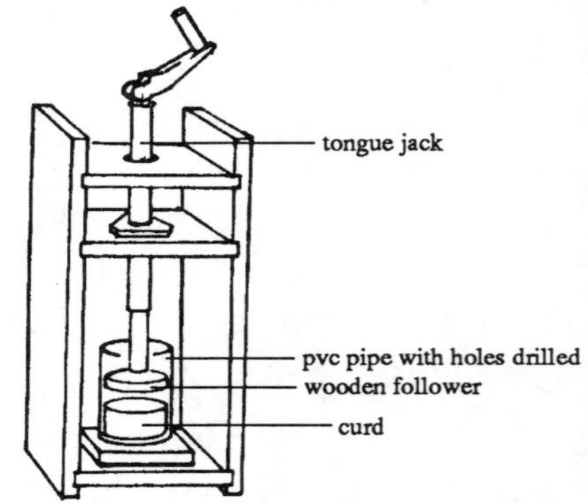

Veggie Treats

Guaranteed Pleasers For Those Who Didn't Think They Liked Them!

In our program we stress the importance of fresh, (or your own home-put-up) vegetables. One of the time-honored "momilies" has been "Eat your vegtables, they're good for you!" Well, you should, and they are! Frequently, we have to sneak vegetables in along with soups, casseroles, and other main dishes, for children have long been at war with the vegetable.

We recommend having a garden of whatever size you are able to manage, for this is one way of enticing children to eat vegetables. They love to pick and eat something they have cared for. The following are just a few of our favorite recipes to make use of your garden's produce.

Marinated Tomatoes

2 Tablespoons fresh snipped, or dried parsley
3 large tomatoes
1/3 Cup vegetable oil
2 Tablespoons minced onion
1 teaspoon each, salt and pepper
1 teaspoon crushed sweet basil
1/4 Cup homemade vinegar
1 clove garlic, crushed

Slice the tomatoes 1/2 inch thick and place in a single layer in a large, shallow dish. Shake in a tightly covered container the following: Oil, salt, pepper, vinegar, and garlic. Pour this mixture over the tomatoes, and sprinkle with the parsley, onion and basil. Cover and refrigerate 3 hours or overnight.

Broccoli Casserole

This is a broccoli dish President Bush would enjoy! Be sure to soak the broccoli in salted water to cover for 20 minutes to draw out any insects that may be present. Rinse well and chop.

3/4 Cup homemade mayonnaise (See index)
3/4 Cup cream of mushroom soup (See index)
4 Cups chopped broccoli
2 teaspoons grated onion
1/2 Cup grated Paramesan cheese
1/2 Cup cracker or bread crumbs
Salt and pepper, to taste

Mix well the ingredients except the crumbs, and put in a casserole dish. Top with the crumbs and bake at 400° for 20 minutes. Serve hot.

Zucchini has been compared to a rabbit. . . both are extremely prolific. The following two recipes will make a zucchini lover out of even the most skeptical, and when you raise zucchini, you need all the zucchini lovers you can muster!

Zucchini n' Bacon

2 small tomatoes, peeled and diced
5-6 small zucchini
3 slices bacon, diced
1 onion, chopped
1 Tablespoon sugar
Seasoned salt and pepper, to taste

Place diced bacon in the bottom of a saucepan that has a tight-fitting lid. (Being on the bottom allows it to cook thoroughly.) Layer the other ingredients on top and cover with the lid. Simmer over medium heat for 15 minutes. Stir before serving. Serves 4

Zucchini and Green Beans

1 Can, or 2 Cups fresh, cut green beans
1 onion, chopped
2 medium zucchini, sliced
1 slice bacon
1/2 teaspoon seasoned salt
1/4 Cup butter or margarine
fresh ground pepper

If using canned beans, drain. If using fresh, cook and drain. Fry bacon until crisp and drain. Crumble and reserve. Wilt onion in the margarine over medium heat. Add zucchini and increase the heat to high. Stir until barely cooked. Combine all the ingredients and heat through. Serves 6

Corn-Stuffed Tomatoes

6 large, fresh tomatoes
2 Cups cooked corn
1/3 Cup chopped celery
1/3 Cup soft bread crumbs
1 teaspoon seasoned salt
1 Cup grated homemade cheese
1 Tablespoon diced pimiento (optional)
1 teaspoon sugar
1/4 Cup chopped onion

Wash tomatoes and cut off the tops. Scoop out the centers, leaving a thick shell. Save the pulp and mix with the other ingredients. Place the tomatoes in a baking dish and fill the cavities with the corn mixture. Bake 20 minutes at 350°. Serves 6. (This mixture is also good when used to stuff zucchini which has been split length-wise and hollowed.)

Eggplant Parmesan

2 Cups homemade spaghetti sauce (See index)
1/4 Cup milk, soy milk or Milk♥Lite®

1 large eggplant
2 tomatoes, sliced
1 teaspoon seasoned salt
Sliced homemade cheese
Oil for frying
3/4 Cups flour
2 eggs, beaten
2-3 twists fresh ground pepper
Grated Parmesan cheese
Parsley for garnish

Wash the eggplant and slice 1/4″ thick. Sprinkle generously with plain salt and let set for 20 minutes to draw out the juices which would make the eggplant mushy. Rinse and pat dry. Mix the flour with the salt and pepper. Dip the slices into the milk, then the flour. Dip them in the beaten egg and into flour once again. Fry in hot oil until golden. Pour the spaghetti sauce into the bottom of a 9″ x 13″ baking pan and lay the eggplant slices on top. Top each with a slice of tomato, followed by cheese. Sprinkle with Parmesan and bake for 15 minutes at 350°. Serves 6 to 8.

Beekeeping - Nature's Sweet Bounty At a Honey of a Price

Taking it easy and having a crew of dedicated workers performing their labor for you is a popular fantasy nearly all of us have entertained at one time or another. Beekeeping offers an opportunity to indulge this fantasy; for while 50,000 to 60,000 workers in a hive literally work themselves to death, you need only spend about 8 hours a year of your time. This 8 hours, plus a moderate investment in equipment should provide all the honey you will need each year.

"BEE"Ginning

Bees and supplies can be mail ordered, and many a beekeeper has gotten his start with the help of a Sears Catalog. At the end of this chapter is a list of suppliers and magazines helpful to the novice and experienced beekeeper alike.

Bees can be kept successfully nearly everywhere, even in the city where their main source of nectar often is potted ornamentals. If you have any questions about the suitability and possible restrictions of your area, contact your local USDA or county agent, (County Extension Services). They can also put you in touch with other beekeepers whose experience is invaluable to a beginner.

Choosing Your Hive Site

Before you obtain your bees, careful consideration should be given to a hive site. In the warmer areas of the South, shade is essential during the heat of the day. In colder climates, it is important that the hive be sheltered from wind and away from low pockets where cold air has a tendency to settle.

Bees collect a lot of water and having a water source nearby will help prevent their gathering around swimming pools, hoses and other inconvenient areas.

Bees tend to make a "bee line" to their nectar source, so try to face the hive opening in that direction. They can forage up to a distance of five miles from the hive, but less toll is taken on them if they locate their nectar within a mile radius. This means the honey output is greater per time and energy expended per bee.

If it is possible, try to orient the hive entrance where the morning sun can warm the bees to activity as soon as possible.

If houses or neighbors are in the line of flight, erect a tall hedge or fence 15 feet or so in front of the hive. This forces their flight higher and lessens the possibility of nuisance.

Finally, keep the hive off the ground where moisture can become a problem. It can cause rot in the wood of the hive, and raise the humidity to a stressful level for the bees whose job it is to ventilate the hive. Concrete blocks or flat rocks will serve to lift the hive.

The Anatomy Of A Hive

The hive should be assembled and ready prior to the arrival of your bees. Looking from the bottom to the top, a hive will consist of: **1. BOTTOM BOARD** which will rest on the previously described concrete blocks or rocks. **2. ENTRANCE REDUCER** permits the hive's opening to be made larger during peak honey flow, or smaller when the reduced honey flow could lead to an invasion from robber bees from a different, stronger colony. A smaller entrance gives the advantage to the guard bees stationed at the entrance. **3.** The **HIVE BODY** proper, usually consists of two larger chambers. This is where the queen lays her eggs and the young, or brood, are raised. Here also, is honey stored to provide food for the colony over the winter. **4.** A **QUEEN EXCLUDER** follows, and its purpose is to restrict the Queen's passage to the upper parts of the hive which are the supers. **5. SUPERS**, there are usually two or more, depending upon the vigor of the colony and the strength of the honey flow. By excluding the Queen from these chambers, the cells formed on the hanging frames inside get filled with surplus honey. This is the honey which is harvested for your use. Topping the supers are the covers. **6. COVERS**, there are two, an inner cover containing a ventilation hole, and an outer, weatherproof one. This completes the structural parts of the hive.

Needed for the bee's use is the wax foundation. While bees can construct their own combs, their arrangement is frequently haphazard and it exacts quite a toll on the bee. In fact, it requires the bees to consume 8 pounds of honey to produce only 1 pound of wax- (an interesting statistic to consider when you desire to produce a lot of comb honey.) Beekeepers, therefore, provide a base - a foundation - upon which the bees construct their combs. For cut comb honey, plain wax foundation is best. This, however, doesn't possess the strength required to stand up to the honey extractor, or even the years of bee workings and human handling. Here is where reinforced foundation is preferred and there are several types you can choose from. They may be obtained from the source list at the end of this chapter.

Now, For The Beekeeper

There are several items needed for the beekeeper's convenience, not the least of which is the **VEIL**. This is the net which, when worn over a wide brimmed **HAT** and tucked securely into a tightly buttoned collar, prevents the bees from getting into your hair or inside your shirt. A **WHITE, LONG-SLEEVED SHIRT** with fitted cuffs and **WHITE LONG PANTS** with cuffs fastened tightly into stout **BOOTS** completes the clothing requirements. There is a division of thought regarding **GLOVES**. Some beekeepers prefer the dexterity that bare hands provide. Also, other bees are stimulated to sting by the scent a bee sting leaves in the glove. (Keep this in mind when handling the bees. Try to avoid crushing any as this would release the scent, or pheromone.) If gloves are chosen, heavy leather ones with elasticized gauntlets are suggested.

Collecting Your Honey

A **HIVE TOOL** is needed for the prying apart of the various hive components. Where a conventional crowbar is too thick and unwieldy, the hive tool is designed for the job.

A **BEE BRUSH** is a soft bristle brush used to sweep the bees from the frame when you are working with them or harvesting the honey. It helps avoid crushing them and when used in a gentle and deliberate manner, they don't seem to object.

A **SMOKER**, preferably of stainless steel, is used to quiet and gentle the bees when it is necessary to enter the hive. Not only does the smoke mask the pheromone which excites the bees, it also causes them to engorge with honey, and with a "full tummy" they are much more placid. (Just try to run a race after Thanksgiving Dinner!)

EXTRACTING EQUIPMENT is where the biggest investment lies. While uncapped combs can be laid across clean pans and allowed to drip, much more honey is obtained with the use of an extractor. Electric models are available along with manually operated ones and the cost varies accordingly. There are even plans available to help you make your own extractor, see the last of this chapter for addresses.

An **UNCAPPING KNIFE** is a long knife which, when heated, aids in cutting off the wax tops of the honey cells, allowing release of the honey. The electric ones are the easiest to use, being kept at a constant temperature without having to reheat.

Establishing Your Bees

With the hive and equipment ready it is time to order the bees. It is best to order them in the early spring so the colony can build up to full strength before the honey flow begins. They will come as a mated Queen, (she needs only to mate once in her lifetime), and about three pounds of attendant workers. While it may seem like a lot of bees, those that accompany the Queen will live only about 6 weeks, providing care of the hive and Queen until the new broods hatch and begin to build up the colony. The Queen comes in a separate box complete with a sugar plug. When introducing her to the hive, do not remove the plug, as the worker bees chew the candy away in a gradual manner. This allows time for the bees to become acclimated to the Queen and her scent, for her particular pheromone binds the hive together. Since the Queen and these temporary workers are not related, she would stand a great chance of being destroyed by them without this gradual introduction.

Feed the bees with the sugar syrup that accompanied the shipment and shake them gently into the waiting hive. Insert the queen box with her attendants and gently close the hive. Any bees left over can be placed, in their shipping container, in front of the hive where they will eventually find their way inside. Remember always to move slowly and gently and your chances of getting stung will be reduced. If you do receive a sting, always scrape the stinger out, never pinch it. Pinching just compresses the venom sac still attached and gives you a more painful sting. Keep in mind the caution regarding crushing bees. When a bee stings, she is mortally wounded and soon dies anyway, so don't bother slapping at her.

On about the third or fifth day, if the weather is nice, gently open the hive and check the Queen cage. If the candy plug is gone, you know that she has been freed. If the plug is intact, carefully make a small hole with a nail, the bees will do the rest. If the plug is gone, remove the box, otherwise wait a couple more weeks before removal.

Resist the temptation to check on the bees more often than once a week. This is especially critical if the weather is cool, for heat lost from an opened hive can greatly stress the bees. In addition, they will consume more honey in an effort to keep themselves and the Queen warm.

During the first month while the colony is getting established, it is a good idea to keep them fed with sugar water you provide. Then when the honey flow is established, you can let your industrious little workers lay up your golden trove.

Swarming

A periodic check during the warm spring months can tell you if the colony is likely to swarm, that is divide and depart with the Queen. If the bees act droopy and crowded on the inner cover, and if there are several peanut shaped Queen cells capped, it is likely they are readying to swarm. Check the brood chambers, if there are anywhere from 5-8 uniform sized and shaped Queen cells, leave them alone, for they are likely to be replacing a dead or dying Queen. If you find over 6 to 20 different sized and irregular cells toward the bottom, they should be removed as they are likely swarm cells.

With the coming of summer, the swarming instinct lessens and you will want to add more brood chambers and/or supers.

The Golden Reward

Home beekeepers usually prefer to harvest the honey after the fall honey flow, just before the frost. With proper swarm management and a strong colony, you might be able to obtain a respectable harvest the first year, although many experts suggest you wait until the second year.

Pick a sunny, calm day to harvest the honey. Bees' temperament is greatly influenced by the weather. Using the smoker and soft bee brush, open the hive and gently clear the frames of bees. Take care not to crush any bees in the process. If the frames are 80% sealed over, they are ready for harvest. Take the frames to a bee-proof, preferably screened room for the extraction process. Using the heated decapping knife, slice the caps from the comb. Drop them into a cheesecloth lined colander for later retrieval of the honey they contain. Place the combs in the extractor and turn it on. If using a manual extractor, spin slowly to avoid damaging the combs. When you have finished, hang the cheesecloth filled with caps and honey over a pan to drain overnight. Return the frames to the hive where the bees will clean them of honey. It generally takes about two to three days for them to complete the task.

The honey you have extracted needs to be strained to remove any dead bees and foreign matter. A two-tiered method works well. Line a sieve or strainer with cheesecloth, previously wrung out in warm water. Over this, place a piece of wire mesh or window screen. When the slightly warmed newly-extracted honey is poured into this arrangement, the larger debris are trapped by the top screen, and the finer by the cheesecloth lined sieve.

Allow the strained honey to stand several days while the air bubbles rise to the top where they may be skimmed off. Some people package it right away in clean glass jars. Others, in an attempt to retard fermentation and crystallization, heat the honey over simmering water to Pasteurize it. Using a candy thermometer, heat to 150°, no hotter or the flavor will be affected. Pour into clean jars and seal. Store your honey in a warm, (80° if possible), dry room. If it crystallizes, it can be returned to liquid form by gently heating over hot water and stirring.

After The Harvest

When the honey harvest is over it is time to make preparations for overwintering the hive. In warmer climates nothing more might be needed than reducing the hive entrance and covering the opening with a piece of hardware cloth to keep the mice out. An insulating layer of hay or straw may be place on the top, contained within a wooden box or shallow super. In colder climates where a snow pack might obscure the bottom board, a ventilating and exit hole must be drilled in the side of the top hive body. A 3/4 inch hole is sufficient. Assure that the bees have sufficient honey and pollen to carry them through the winter, or supplement them with winter feedings of sugar syrup in a 2 parts sugar to one part water ratio. Wrap the hive securely with tarpaper, and staple leaving the vent hole free. Never cover the hive with an impermeable material like plastic. The humid air within needs to escape to avoid frost build-up inside.

With the arrival of spring, it is time to remove the tarpaper and the whole process begins all over again.

Preventing Disease

No discussion of bees is complete without mentioning the most serious of bee diseases, American Foulbrood. This is a bacterial disease which affects the bee larvae within their sealed cells, slowly turning them into a slimy, smelly goo. It is found worldwide and there is no known cure. The spores formed by the bacterium are so resistant they survive freezing and even the most thorough scouring with soap and disinfectants. They are found on the bees, comb, honey, even within the very wood of the hive, itself.

The seriousness of this disease warrants a thorough checking of the brood chambers at least once a year. Healthy cells will have slightly bulging caps, be intact and of a pale golden color throughout. If American Foulbrood is present, caps will be discolored, wet and sunken. They will frequently contain irregularly chewed holes and have a foul order. A simple and certain test is to insert a small stick through several suspect cells. If the goo contained within adheres to the stick and stretches in a thick, rubbery manner before it snaps, you can be certain it is American Foulbrood.

This virulent disease is easily transmitted among hives, either through bee to bee contact when foraging or robbing, or coming in contact with honey or contaminated hive material. Having no cure, the only control is to gas the bees after nightfall when all the foragers have returned home. The frames have to be burned and everything else well-charred with a blowtorch, or burned. The devastation wreaked by this disease is so great that most areas have laws that authorize the bee inspector to burn any infected hive he comes across.

The Treatment

Do not let the severity of American Foulbrood dissuade you from enjoying the pleasures beekeeping offers. Fortunately, it can be prevented with the antibiotic Terramycin. It is easily obtained at feed stores or from veterinarians. You do not want it to contaminate honey used for human consumption, so treat early in the spring, at least 4 weeks before the first honeyflow, and then in the fall, after the honey harvest.

A bright yellow powder, Terramycin comes in several strengths. It is administered to the bees by mixing with powdered sugar and you will want to carefully read the package instructions to obtain the right concentration. You will want 200 milligrams per every 3 Tablespoons, (one ounce), of sugar. To administer, just place one ounce on a piece of cardboard or paper. Terramycin is toxic to the bee larvae, so take care not to spill it. Gently place the paper on top of the frames in one corner. The bees, in the course of feeding their young, will pass the right amount to the brood. Two more doses should be given at four day intervals.

This simple preventive measure should exempt you from the consequences of Foulbrood, but if you should ever come across it, immediate destruction of the colony is necessary.

Beekeeping brings many joys, not the least of which is the delicious honey you and your 60,000 servants have produced. You will become comfortable and proficient in your management but, if for whatever reason, the time may come when you decide you no longer wish to be a beekeeper, please be responsible and remember how serious is the threat of disease to other beekeepers.

Never abandon your hives, where through neglect, they could become a repository of disease. An ad placed in the local paper should bring an eager response from someone anxious to give beekeeping a try. If that fails, however, gas the bees and bury them, complete with the combs and frames.

How Sweet It Is

With your success as a producer of your own honey, you will find yourself experimenting with the use of this ancient sweetener. In most cases it can replace either white or brown sugar. Being composed of glucose and fructose, as compared to sugar's sucrose, it is generally sweeter and of course has a higher moisture content. Therefore, you would replace approximately half of the sugar with honey and reduce the liquid in the recipe by 1/4 Cup.

Honey absorbs and retains moisture easily, thus making cookies chewier and keeping breads and other baked goods moist longer. It also helps baked goods brown easier, so to avoid over-browning, reduce the oven temperature by 25°.

Honey can act, not only as a sweetener, but as a seasoning in its own right. Root vegetables benefit from a touch of honey, as does poultry and some meats. Who hasn't enjoyed the taste of a slice of honey-glazed ham?

Honeys are not all the same. Depending upon the predominant source of nectar, they can range from the reddish brown Australian Eucalyptus honey with a pronounced tang, to Acacia honey which is almost clear and delicately sweet. As a general rule of thumb, the darker the color of the honey, the more strongly flavored it will be.

In her whole 6 week lifespan, a worker bee will produce about 1/12 of a teaspoon of honey. It takes nearly 2 million flowers to produce the nectar required for 1 pound of honey.

If you desire to make jam without the use of white sugar, try boiling 2 quarts of fresh fruit until it has reduced and thickened. Stir in 1/2 Cup of honey and pour into jars and freeze.

The following is a list of Suppliers and magazines which may be of help to you:

American Bee Supply, Inc.
P. O. Box 555 Rt. 7 Sparta Pike
Lebanon TN 37088-0555

Gleanings in Bee Culture
A good magazine for
the backyard beekeeper.
623 West Liberty Street
P. O. Box 706
Medina, OH 44258-0706

Cumberland General Store Catalog
A fascinating catalog . . .
R. 3, Box 81,Crossville, TN 38555

Keeping Bees by John Vivian
An excellent, in-depth bookwith numerous
photographs. Great for the beginner.
Williamson Publishing Co.
Charlotte, VT 01986

Storey's ***Books for Country Living***
Has plans for building your own extractor and hives, etc.
Dept 9317 Schoolhouse Road
Pownal, VT 05261

The Leftover Question

We grew up in homes where the motto was: "Make over, make do, or do without." Nothing was ever thrown away that couldn't be utilized in some fashion; be it redesigned clothing, or redesigned dinners.

In this chapter we will present a few ideas that will enable you to really make this program work for you. As you have probably surmised by now, one of the keys to its successful implementation is **PREPLANNING**. Recipes using leftovers are helpful, but even more so is a whole new (to some) philosophy: **THINK BEFORE THROWING**.

Here are just a few tips and, as you get the feel, you will no doubt develop some ideas of your own.

1. **LIQUIDS** from **COOKED** or **CANNED VEGETABLES** are full of vitamins, minerals, and flavor. Collect them in a jar in the refrigerator or freezer until enough is accumulated. It is good added to **SOUPS** or used as the liquid when making **GRAVY**.

   The **WATER** left from cooking **POTATOES**, or for that matter, any left over **POTATOES** themselves, makes a tasty addition to **YEAST BREADS**.

2. By the same token, any leftover **VEGETABLES** or **MEAT SCRAPS** are collected and saved to go into the **SOUP POT**. The French keep a stock pot simmering on the back of the stove and during the day various tidbits and peelings are tossed in. It provides a nutritious soup at the day's end, and the character of the soup changes from day to day. Save well-washed **PEELINGS**, and **ONION SKINS** for color.

3. **MEAT SCRAPS** may be recycled as **HASH** - always a tried and true standby - but may also come forth as hearty **SOUPS** and tasty **SANDWICH SPREADS**. Even **CONSOMME** and **BOUILLON**, which form the basis for many an entreé, can be made from meat scraps. Save them in the freezer in a plastic bag until you have accumulated enough.

   Don't forget the **BONES**. They can be covered with cold water and simmered to extract the flavor. **SMOKED** type meats are best suited for **PEA** and **BEAN SOUPS**, while the others are used in any other soup.

4. **SYRUPS** from fresh or canned **FRUITS** make colorful **ICE CUBES** and impart a delicious flavor to **LEMONADE** or other **FRUIT DRINKS**.

They can also be sweetened and boiled down to make **PANCAKE SYRUPS**. **PEELINGS** and **CORES** are saved and thrown into the **VINEGAR CROCK**, along with any **JAM JAR RINSINGS**, where they develop into delicious **VINEGARS**, the likes of which cannot be found in any store.

5. **EGG WHITES** are never thrown away, for they so easily become **MERINGUES** or **PUDDINGS**. When added to **SCRAMBLED EGGS**, they act as an **EXTENDER** and lower the cholesterol percentage. Blended with a little water, they make a nice **GLAZE** for **YEAST BREADS** before baking. Leftover **YOLKS** can be poached in water and forced through a sieve to add colorful interest to **CREAMED DISHES**, **SALADS** or **SOUPS**. Leftover **SCRAMBLED EGGS** can be chilled and cut into cubes to be added to soups.
6. **DRY BREAD** is a veritable gold mine of possibilities. From **FRENCH TOAST** to **CROUTONS**, **BREAD PUDDINGS** to **CRUMB COATINGS**, to **THICKEN GRAVIES** ... the list goes on. Dry in a paper bag to minimize molding and crush with a rolling pin or in a food processor. Store in a tightly covered jar or tin.
7. **SOUR MILK** can be interchanged with **BUTTERMILK** in all kinds of baking. It adds a tenderness to the crumb, and enhances **PANCAKES**, **CORNBREAD** and **BISCUITS**.
8. **LEMON** and **ORANGE RINDS** are saved in a plastic bag in the freezer where it is a simple matter to grind them, frozen, in the food grinder. Package in foil packets of 1 Tablespoon and keep in a baggie in the freezer. When needed to add flavor to **CAKE BATTERS**, **MUFFIN BATTERS**, **BANANA BREAD**, **RAISIN BREAD**, **WHIPPED CREAM**, **FROSTINGS**, **PUDDINGS**, or **MERINGUES**, just thaw in a little warm water and squeeze out the excess water. If you prefer, they can be dried and grated.
9. **FAT SCRAPS** are saved in the freezer (to prevent rancidity), and used in the making of delightful **SOAPS** and **SHAMPOOS**. (See the "Make-Up And More" section.)

As you can see from the few tips above, thinking before throwing makes good sense. By monitoring what is in the refrigerator and consideration when meal planning, the budget can really be stretched and no one but you need be the wiser. Just think, you never again need hear that old refrain: "Yuck! Leftovers, again?"

The following are a few recipes to help you out. These recipes are simply a guide and may vary with whatever you have on hand and in whatever quantities you've accumulated.

*Note:See **SOUP** section for instructions on making vegetable soup stock from leftover peels and scraps.

Vegetable Soup

3 Tablespoons butter or margarine
1 large onion, chopped
2-3 stalks & leaves celery, chopped
4 carrots, chopped
2-3 chopped tomatoes
1 turnip, chopped
1 1/2 Cups cut lettuce leaves
2 sprigs parsley
1/2 teaspoon dried thyme
1/4 teaspoon pepper
1 1/2 teaspoons seasoned salt
1 clove garlic, minced
1 teaspoon Worcestershire sauce

Melt butter or margarine in a large pot. Add the next seven ingredients and cover. Cook over low heat until the vegetables are tender, about 40 to 45 minutes, stirring occasionally. Add remaining ingredients and cover with 6 1/2 Cups cold water. Bring to a boil, reduce heat and simmer for 2 1/2 hours. If desired, about 1/2 hour before soup is done, 1/2 Cup barley, raw rice, or cooked leftover rice or pasta may be added.

Sandwich Fillings

Grind any leftover meats and add mayonnaise or salad dressing to spreading consistency. Season with chopped pickles, chopped hardboiled eggs, or creamed horseradish.

Meringues

3 egg whites
1 Cup sugar
1/4 teaspoon cream of tartar

Beat the whites until foamy, then add the cream of tartar. Continue beating while adding the sugar gradually. Beat until stiff and glossy. Cut open a brown paper sack and place it on a baking sheet. Place 8 mounds of the meringue on the paper and with the back of a spoon, make a depression in each. Bake at 275°s for 1 hour. Turn off the oven and let them finish drying as the oven cools. Fill with ice cream and your favorite topping, or with sweetened fruit and whipped cream. These freeze very well, unfilled. You do not need to thaw them before using. Makes 8.

Vinegar

Vinegar making is a project that brings great satisfaction, for vinegar is simply the end result of spoilage. It takes no skills and uses material which is normally thrown away. When foods high in sugar, such as honey or fruit juices spoil, or ferment, alcohol is the result. Allow the reaction to continue and vinegar is obtained. Requiring little attention during the process, free scraps become a useful product. By steeping favorite herbs in the finished vinegar, or by using different fruits, delicious variations that would command a premium price in the gourmet shops can be had for practically no cost.

Save Those Peelings

A basic vinegar can be made by placing peelings, cores, and bruised or soft fruit in a gallon glass jar, earthenware crock or similar container. Fill with water to a level of 4 to 6 inches above the surface and add about 3/4 cup of sugar, brown sugar, or molasses. Rinsings from honey or jam jars also benefit the vinegar crock. Cover the crock with a cloth to permit the vinegar to breathe and just set it aside, out of the way, to complete its action. It will ferment, smell like spoiled fruit, and then, after awhile take on the heady fragrance of vinegar. This may take anywhere from 4 to 6 months.

Do not be alarmed at the thick, rubbery scum that will form on the top. This is what is known as the "mother" and is perfectly normal. Save some of it and use it as a "starter" for the next batch of vinegar and the time required will be shortened considerably.

Another fact about vinegar that some may find disturbing is the presence of little fruit flies about the crock. Once again, they are normal. In fact an old time name for a fruit fly was vinegar fly. Just strain them out when you filter the vinegar into the bottles and take comfort in the fact they are a "clean fly", that is, not carrion eaters.

If you plan to keep the vinegar for some length of time, Pasteurization might be desired. This will halt the formation of "mother" when stored in the bottle. It will not, however, be suitable for starting a new batch. To Pasteurize, heat the vinegar to 145° and hold at that temperature for 30 minutes. Cool and bottle.

Soup Base (Beef, Pork, Or Chicken)

Another great way to utilize throw-aways is in the making of soup bases and bouillon cubes. This is integral to our program; in the making of wheat meats and as a flavor enhancer in many of our recipes. While commercial soup bases are available, and there are many delicious ones on the market, the cheapest way is to make your own. If you don't find this possible, look for soup bases in restaurant supply houses, bulk food stores, or food specialty stores, or failing that, check the yellow pages of the telephone directory.

Other Uses

Soup base is useful for more than just soups and wheat meat. Once you begin using it, you will be amazed at its versatility and will wonder how you managed without it before. The beef flavor is especially delicious in sauces of all kinds, to augment stews and casseroles; pot pies and vegetables; hash; dumplings and spreads; noodles and rice; even sour cream based dips.

The chicken flavor finds use in certain molded salads, vegetables and pot pies; stuffed eggs and creamed dishes; pastas and rice; biscuits and dumplings; dips and spreads; gravies and sauces; poached eggs; curries; almost any skillet dishes; pilafs and casseroles; and even in the water used when cooking corn.

When cooking up a pot of green or yellow split peas, the addition of ham or even pork soup base can give the taste of meat when ham hock is not available. In the same light, almost any pot of beans finds benefit in the addition of a little soup base. The only caution, as stated before, is to watch the amount of salt used, as various brands differ in the degree of saltiness.

Homemade Soup Base

To make soup base, collect fat scraps, trimmings, bones and meat scraps. They may sometimes be obtained from the butcher. Save them in a plastic bag in the freezer until approximately 5 to 7 pounds have accumulated. Also save any pan drippings and crusty bits from roasting meats; loosen with a minimum of hot water and scrape them into a jar kept in the refrigerator for that purpose.

When ready to make the stock, place the scraps in a roasting pan which has been oiled with 2 to 3 Tablespoons of vegetable oil. Add two big onions, cut in chunks, one clove garlic, and two Tablespoons parsley. Brown in 450° oven for 50 to 60 minutes stirring occasionally. (For poultry, omit the browning step.)

Transfer the contents to a heavy stockpot, or a slow cooker. Wash the roasting pan out with two cups of water, adding it to the stockpot. At this time add whatever drippings you have accumulated in the refrigerator, first removing the cake of fat at the top.

Simmer gently for eight hours, skimming the scum as it develops.

Strain through a cloth, then chill. When the fat has solidified on the top, discard it and return the stock to the pot. Once again, simmer and when the material coats a metal spoon, remove it from the heat. It should be firm and rubbery after cooling. Keep it stored in the refrigerator.

To make a cup of soup from this base, put one Tablespoon of base in a cup with 1/4 teaspoon salt. Add one cup of boiling water. For variety, a pinch of home dehydrated vegetable flakes can be added.

For people on a salt restricted diet, this soup base has an advantage over the commercial product. When using commercial brands, be sure to adjust the salt to taste, as the degree of saltiness can vary even within the same brand.

Bouillon Cubes

These have the advantage of requiring no refrigeration. To make them, simply remelt the jelly from the above recipe and pour into a loaf pan. Let stand until cool. Cut into 1/2 inch cubes, (equal 1/2 Tablespoon each) and dry in oven or dehydrator at 100°. Wrap in foil or store in a tightly capped jar on the cupboard shelf.

Gelatin

Homemade gelatin is the clarified, unseasoned, meat stock derived from the bony pieces of pork or beef. While beef and pork have the mildest flavor, gelatin made from chicken retains some of the chicken flavor and requires more intense flavoring to mask it.

Cover the bones, (leg, feet, and back pieces yield the stiffest gel) with water and cook at least four hours, or until liquid is reduced by one half. Strain through a cloth and chill. Remove the fat from the top, and scrape the sediment from the bottom.

To clarify, beat 4 to 5 egg whites. Add with the crushed shells to one quart of the homemade gelatin in a saucepan. Let melt over medium heat and once melted, stir. Bring to a boil and boil 10 minutes. Add 1/3 cup cold water and boil 5 more minutes. Remove from heat and cover pan. Let sit ten minutes then strain through a cloth previously wrung out in hot water, (to prevent the gel setting in the fabric.) Squeeze the cloth to remove all the gelatin and refilter if not clear enough. It is difficult to get as clear as commercial gelatin, yet the flavor is far superior.

To use as unflavored gelatin in recipes, substitute two cups of homemade for every envelope of powdered, and decrease the liquid required.

For dessert or salad gelatin, you may use fruit juice concentrates or even powdered soft drink mixes. Sweeten to taste, generally 1/2 to 3/4 cup of sugar to one quart of gelatin. Add the powdered mix to taste, or use lemon juice. Four to five lemons to a quart produces a nice lemon flavor, but can be adjusted to individual preferences.

Keep well chilled, as it melts readily at room temperature.

Make Up Your Own Make-up, and more. . .

This book has thus far dealt with saving money on groceries. Actually, for most of us, a considerable amount of grocery money is spent on non-food items.

In the Miscellaneous chapter you will learn how to make cleaning supplies and laundry soaps, but in this chapter, we will discuss the making of a fine complexion bar. This is not the harsh, brown bar of our grandmother's, but rather, delicately tinted, fragrant soap worthy of any expensive boutique. (See, not only can you feed a family of our for as low as $10.00 a week, but you can give fine gifts, too!)

Shampoo, deodorant, bath soap, toothpaste. . . all add up at the cash register, yet are so simple to make and cost much less.

These are all necessities, but one doesn't have to be austere on our program. There is room for lightheartedness, too. One could argue the merits of cosmetics, but something like make-up which gives the self-image a boost, or fine fragrances to lift the heart, certainly deserve a place alongside some of the necessities.

Marlynn's daughters, Venecia and Jenny, are frequently complimented on their fresh, natural appearance and people are amazed when told it is aided by make-up they've custom blended in the kitchen.

Space, in this book does not permit all the recipes and techniques we have for soap, the making of your own lye, or make-up products. Please refer to ***A Bite Of Independence*** for further recipes and procedures. Following is a recipe which yields one bar, which will, if you pardon the pun, let you slide into soap making gradually.

Making Soap

1. Fat scraps normally thrown away are melted over low heat, or in a pan in a low oven. (The whitest soap is made from clean fat from butchering.) This recipe uses beef fat. Strain through several layers of cheese cloth to remove impurities. You will need 1 Cup.

2. Assemble materials and equipment: <u>LYE</u>, not Drāno, can be found in most hardware stores and supermarkets near the cleaning supplies; 2 heat-resistant plastic, stainless steal, enamel, glass or earthenware containers for

mixing the soap and dissolving the lye; a good thermometer; rubber gloves; wooden or stainless steel spoon for stirring; Borax; and soft, or distilled water. **Eye protectors are advisable,** and if you want colored soap, a piece of old crayon.

CAUTION: This is a CAUSTIC PROCESS. Keep AWAY from CHILDREN and HANDLE THE LYE VERY CAREFULLY. Do not SPLASH or GET IN THE EYES. If it gets on the skin, WASH OFF IMMEDIATELY with cool water. IF IN THE EYES, SEEK MEDICAL HELP.

Standard Bar soap Recipe (1 Bar)

1 Cup melted fat
1/2 Cup soft water
small piece of wax crayon
5 teaspoons lye
1 teaspoon borax

Shave the piece of crayon into the fat so that they melt together. Have the fat at 95° to 100°. Dissolve the lye in cold water and add the borax. The lye generates a lot of heat, take care. Cool the lye to 95° to 100°.

In a thin, steady stream pour the warm fat solution into the lye, stirring evenly and steadily. Continue stirring steadily until the soap reaches a creamy honey-like consistency. This will take approximately 30 minutes.

If the soap fails to thicken, place the container in cold water to stir. If it gets lumpy, place it in hot water and stir to dissolve the lumps. If the soap appears greasy, or has crumbly texture, add a little water and re-dissolve it over low heat.

When the consistency is thick and creamy, pour into a mold to set. (A mold can be a small cardboard box, a custard cup, or similar small container. Line boxes with plastic wrap or waxed paper. Spray rigid molds with nonstick spray.)

The soap cannot be used right away, it needs a period of at least two weeks to cure. The longer it cures, the harder and longer keeping it becomes. The easiest way to scent the soap is to place it next to a cotton ball touched with your favorite perfume. There are other ways, all described in A Bite Of Independence, but none seem as successful.

Herbal Shampoo

3 Tablespoons each, Rosemary, Parsley, Sage, and Thyme
3 Cups of boiling water

Place the herbs in the boiling water and let steep for 2 hours. Strain and use as follows:

2 Ounces shaved bar soap 3 Cups boiling herbal water
2 Ounces Vodka (add for use for oily hair)

Dissolve the soap in the boiling herbal water. Boil gently until it is dissolved. Cool and if making the oily-hair formula, add vodka. Whip and store in a tightly covered container. Note: If the problem is not oily hair, but rather, dry, flaky scalp, mix 2 parts homemade vinegar to 1 part water and rub into the scalp after the shampoo. Rinsing is optional.

Soybean Whey Shampoo

While not actually a soap, the whey remaining from tofu-making (See the Soybean section), has remarkable shampoo properties. The lecithin contained in the oils has the ability to cut through oil and grease, leaving the hair shiny and soft. Although no suds are formed, it none-the-less performs an excellent job of cleaning.

Lipstick

1/4 teaspoon beeswax
1 teaspoon olive or vegetable oil
7 drops vegetable food coloring, color of your choice

Melt the beeswax and oil over low heat, watching carefully. Stir in the food color. This has the tendency to separate, so stir vigorously until it cools. Put into a small container and apply with a lipstick brush

Blush or Facial Powder

This is the same formula for both products. The difference between them lies in the choice of colors.

1 teaspoon talc
1 Tablespoon cornstarch
1/8 teaspoon vegetable or olive oil
Food color of your choice*

* amount depending upon intensity desired.

Blend together and put in an appropriate container. Apply with fingertips, or cosmetic brush.

Toothpaste

2 ounces salt
2 ounces baking soda
1 Tablespoon glycerine
Water
Few drops of peppermint oil, wintergreen, or other flavoring of your choice

Mix together in a small bowl, adding sufficient water to make a paste. Pack into a small squeeze bottle for use.

Miscellaneous

Every book needs a "Catch-all" chapter; a "Too late to classify..." chapter as it were. Well, this is it. Here you will find laundry soap, cleaning supplies, and yes, even spice mixes and hints. Sort of like an old-fashioned general store that offered everything from pickles to hair cuts, this chapter is.

Laundry Soap

Making soap entails the use of lye, a very caustic material. Take extreme care not to breathe the fumes or splash. Please review the directions for making soap in the "Make-up and More" section.

In a plastic, stainless steel, earthen-ware or granite container, stir the following:

11 Cups cold distilled or soft water **1 Can of lye**

Dissolve lye in the cold water, stirring with a wooden or stainless steel spoon, let cool to barely warm.

<u>Add:</u> 11 Cups warm, rendered fat
1/2 Cup sudsing ammonia
1/2 Cup Sal Soda, (optional)
1 Cup Borax
1 Cup household liquid bleach

Stir, then let set. Repeat this procedure until the mixture gets thick and crumbly. This could take an entire day. As it becomes difficult to work, it helps to don the rubber gloves and crumble with the hands. Spreading the mixture on a newspaper and crumbling it daily helps to further dry it until it resembles the fine particles of the commercial product. (When fully dry you can put it through a food processor to powder it.)

• **<u>TO USE YOUR HOMEMADE LAUNDRY SOAP</u>**: Use very hot water and add the soap to the water prior to the clothes. Use 1½ Cups per load and agitate briefly to assure the soap's dissolving. (Our forebears used the same water for several loads, washing the lightest articles first, and progressing through to the darker and more soiled clothes. In this case, 3 Cups of soap were used.) You will find that using homemade soap leaves the clothes with a delightful, clean fragrance.

• **<u>CLEANING THE WASHER</u>**: You will find the use of homemade soap requires the periodic cleaning of the washer to rid it of built up minerals and deposits. Simply fill it with warm water and add 1 Cup of homemade vinegar. Run it through the cycle and that is all there is to it. It should be done once a month.

Bluing

When a little bluing is added to the last rinse water, whites come out looking much whiter. This is due to the sunlight reflecting back from the blue, giving the illusion of whiteness. Bluing is especially helpful to use with homemade laundry soap which lacks the many additives found in commercial products.

1 Ounce Prussian Blue powder (available from the pharmacy)
1/2 Ounce powdered oxalic acid (available from the pharmacy)
1 Quart soft, or distilled, water

Mix together and store on the laundry shelf. (A couple of drops added to the rinse water when shampooing grey hair will help whiten it - do not use too much and have blue hair.) (Recommended by the groomer for shampooing the author's Schnauzer dog to whiten its coat.)

Spice Mixes and Other Things

Curry Powder

1/3 Cup coriander seed
1 1/2 teaspoon cardamon seed
1 teaspoon black peppercorns
3 small bay leaves
1 teaspoon ground ginger
1/4 Cup ground turmeric
1 Tablespoon whole cumin
6 Whole cloves
1 1/2 sticks of cinnamon

Combine all the ingredients and roast for 25 minutes in a 200° oven. Stir occasionally. Grind to a fine powder with a mortar and pestle, or use the blender. Makes approximately 3/4 Cup. Store in an airtight jar on the cupboard shelf.

Seasoning Salt

1 1/4 Cup salt
2 Tablespoons sugar
2 Tablespoons black pepper
2 teaspoons garlic salt
1/4 teaspoon curry powder
1 Tablespoon celery salt
2 teaspoons onion salt
2 teaspoons dry mustard
1 Tablespoon paprika
1 teaspoon fine dry parsley

Mix together and keep in the cupboard. Makes about 1 1/2 Cups.

Sausage Seasoning

With a touch of this blend, wheat meat takes in a whole new dimension!

2 1/2 Tablespoons rubbed or ground sage
2 Tablespoons rosemary
2 Tablespoons marjoram
1/2 teaspoon dry onion flakes
2 Tablespoons sweet basil
1/2 teaspoon dry minced garlic
1/8 teaspoon cayenne pepper

Blend together and store in an airtight jar on the cupboard.

Worcestershire Sauce

$2^1/_2$ Tablespoons homemade catsup
1/2 teaspoon ground cloves
1 teaspoon anchovy paste
1 Tablespoon raisins
3 green onions, minced
1 quart homemade vinegar

Mix all together in the top of a double boiler. Heat through, stirring to assure even mixing. Remove from heat and cover. Let stand two days, undisturbed, then strain. If not clear, repeat the straining. Pour into a bottle and store, tightly covered, in the refrigerator. Makes nearly 1 quart.

"Falcon-Brand" Condensed Milk

1 Cup hot water
1/3 Cup light corn syrup
2 Cups dry powdered milk
pinch of salt
1/2 Cup soft butter or margarine
$1^2/_3$ Cups sugar
1/4 teaspoon vanilla

Put the water, corn syrup and sugar in a blender with the vanilla and salt. Blend until smooth. Gradually add the soft (use very soft) butter or margarine, taking care to scrape and blend evenly. When smooth, put in a covered container and chill at least 12 hours before using. Yields about 3 Cups. This freezes well.

Basic Bread Stuffing Mix

This is the stuffing we use when serving wheat meat "turkey" or "chicken" and gravy dinners. It also goes well with fish or beef.

1 small chopped onion
1/4 Cup chopped celery
2 Cups cubed dry bread
1/8 teaspoon dried sage
3 Tablespoons margarine
1 teaspoon soup base of choice, to taste
1/2 Cup boiling water

Sauté onion and celery in margarine in a small saucepan. Add soup base and water, simmer to dissolve. Sprinkle sage over dry bread and stir in the water mixture. When evenly moistened, serve as is, or bake, covered, in a greased dish for 35 to 40 minutes at 350°. Makes 2 cups. Can be doubled or increased as needed.

Spices & Herbs

(See Tables on following 4 pages for their uses.)

Spices & Herbs - Table 1

Spice	Appetizers	Soups	Salads & Dressings	Vegetables
Allspice	relishes, pickles, cocktail meatballs, pickled beets, fruit compote	vegetable beef, pea, minestrone, tomato, asparagus	cottage cheese, fruit salad, cheese dressing	eggplant, beets, spinach, squash, red cabbage, turnips, zucchini
Bay Leaves	hot tomato juice, pickles, pickled beets	Bouillon, fish chowders, potato, lobster bisque, bouillabaisse	French dressing, beet salad, seafood salad, tomato & chicken aspic	carrots, rice, beets, lentils, artichokes, potatoes, zucchini, eggplant, onions
Caraway	soft cheese spreads, pickles	cream soups, clam chowder, borscht, vegetable	spiced vinegar, cole slaw, potato salad, sour cream dressing	cabbage, cauliflower, potatoes, turnips, Brussels sprouts, sauerkraut, onions
Cayenne	deviled eggs, seafood sauces, cottage & cream cheese dips & spreads, avocado dip	clam & oyster stews, fish chowder, shrimp gumbo, vegetable	tuna, shrimp, chicken, macaroni, mayonnaise, Thousand Island dressing, sour cream	Lima beans, cut corn, kale, broccoli, green beans
Saffron		lobster bisque, turkey, chicken, bouillabaisse	seafood salads	rice
Sage	cheese spreads	fish and corn chowders, cream of tomato, turkey	salad dressings, green salad	tomatoes, carrots, Brussels sprouts, squash, peas
Sesame Seed	soft cheeses	most soups	salad dressings, cole slaw	asparagus, green beans, eggplant, rice, potatoes
Tarragon	vegetable juice cocktail, stuffed eggs, herb butter, pickled, seafood cocktails	tomato, consommé bean, turtle, pea, mushroom, seafood chowders, chicken	celery, chicken, asparagus, cucumber, egg, cole slaw, green & kidney bean	broccoli, spinach, beans, celery, cabbage, cauliflower, mushrooms
Celery Seed	deviled eggs, ham spread, kraut juice, tomato juice, pickles	cream of celery and tomato, fish chowders, potato, vegetable, bean	potato, tuna, egg, cole slaw, vegetables, sour cream dressing	cabbage, stewed tomatoes, cauliflower, potatoes, turnips, braised lettuce
Chili Powder	avocado dips, cheese dips, seafood cocktail sauce	corn soup, fish & clam chowder, bean, shrimp gumbo, chili	Thousand Island dressing, French dressing, chili sauce	relishes, green peas, eggplant, rice, tomatoes, green beans, corn
Cinnamon	toast, pickled fruits, sweet gherkins, hot spiced beverages		fruit salad, dressing for fruit salad	sweet potatoes, squash, pumpkins, spinach, turnips, parsnips, beets

Spices & Herbs - Table 2

Spice	Eggs & Cheese	Meat & Sauces	Poultry & Fish	Baked Goods
Allspice	cream cheese, egg casserole	beef stew, meat loaf, hamburgers, cranberry sauce, gravies, tomato sauce	boiled fish, chicken, oyster stew	mincemeat, spice cake, tapioca & chocolate puddings
Bay Leaves	Eggs creole	meat pie, corned beef, pot roast, lamb, veal spare ribs, gravies	capon, chicken à la king, boiled fish, lobster, shrimp	
Caraway	cheese soufflé, cottage cheese	sauerbraten, roast beef, liver, kidney stew	tuna fish casserole, roast goose	rye bread, muffins, rolls, cookies, loaf & coffee cakes
Cayenne	boiled and fried eggs, cheese soufflé	pork chops, veal stew, barbecued beef, meat sauces	creamed chicken & croquettes, oysters, tuna salad	
Saffron	scrambled eggs	roast turkey, veal, rabbit, gravy for chicken	bouillabaisse, arroz con pollo, stews, seafood	breads, rolls, buns cake, icings
Sage	soufflés, cream cheese, cheese sauces	beef, pork, veal, lamb, stews, barbecue, meat pies	goose, duck, capon chicken stuffing	
Sesame Seed	cream cheese	Hawaiian ham, meat pies	fish, fried chicken, chicken casseroles	toppings for pies, rolls, cookies, cakes, crumpets
Tarragon	omelets, deviled eggs, scrambled eggs, cottage cheese	meat marinades, pot roast, lamb, gravies	chicken, duck, turkey, seafood dishes	
Celery Seed	boiled & fried eggs, cheese sauce, omelets, casseroles deviled eggs,	meat loaf, pot roast, stews, short ribs	fish stews, chicken croquettes, oysters, stufffings	salt breads, rolls, biscuits
Chili Powder	casseroles, omelets, soufflés, scrambled & boiled eggs, rarebits	chili con carne, arroz con pollo, tamales, meat loaf, hamburgers	shrimp, arroz con pollo, creamed seafood	Mexican-style corn bread
Cinnamon	French toast	pork chops, ham, sauce for pork or lamb	boiled fish and chicken	apple desserts, cakes, puddings, molassses cookies

Spices & Herbs - Table 3

Spice	Appetizers	Soups	Salads & Dressings	Vegetables
Cloves	fruit punch, hot spiced wines, sweet gherkins, pickled fruits	beef, bean, cream of tomato, cream of pea, mulligatawaney	topping for fruit salad	baked beans, squash, beets, candied sweet potatoes
Curry Powder	sauce for dips, sweet pickles, tomato juice, salted nuts, deviled eggs	clam & fish chowders, oyster stew, tomato, mushroom	fruit & meat salads, French dressing, mayonnaise	rice, creamed onions, scalloped tomatoes, carrots, corn, celery, lima beans
Paprika	deviled eggs, cream cheese dips, canapés, seafood cocktails	cream soups, chicken soup, chowders	cole slaw, potato, mayonnaise, French dressing	cauliflower, celery, potatoes, creamed vegetables
Poppy Seed	cheese spreads, cottage cheese, cheese dips	onion soup	green salads, salad dressing	peas, potatoes, sweet potatoes, zucchini, rutabaga
Rosemary	deviled eggs, sour cream dips, pickles	mock turtle, lentil, minestrone, spinach, split pea, chicken	fruit salad, meat salad	potatoes, mushrooms, peas, lima beans, green beans, broccoli
Dill	stuffed eggs, cottage cheese, anchovy spread, pickles, sour cream dips	split pea, navy bean, lobster bisque, borscht, fish	cole slaw, sour cream, cucumber, mayonnaise, seafood, dressings	carrots, beets, cabbage, green beans, zucchini, cauliflower, lima beans, turnips
Ginger	pickles, boiled grapefruit, chutney	bean soup, onion, potato	ginger pears, French dressing	beets, carrots, squash, baked beans
Marjoram	fruit punch, cottage cheese dips, cheddar cheese spread, pickles	clam, oyster, Boston clam chowder, onion, minestrone, oxtail	asparagus, chicken, green salad, fruit, seafood	carrots, eggplant, spinach, string beans, tomatoes, celery, broccoli, summer squash
Mustard	deviled eggs, pickled onions, pickles, Chinese hot sauce, ham spreads	lobster bisque, bean, onion	egg salad, shrimp, lobster, potato, salad dressings	asparagus, beets, Brussels sprouts, broccoli, potatoes, baked beans, green beans, cabbage
Oregano	vegetable juice, avocado dip, pizza, cheese spreads, cottage cheese	bean, beef, tomato, lentil, spinach, onion, navy bean	seafood, avocado, salad dressings, potato, tomato, green beans	peas, onions, green beans, stewed tomatoes, mushrooms, potatoes, spinach

Spices & Herbs - Table 4

Spice	Eggs & Cheese	Meat & Sauces	Poultry & Fish	Baked Goods
Cloves		baked ham, pork roast, stews, gravies, boiled tongue, sausage	baked fish, chicken à la king, roast or smothered chicken	preserves, stewed fruits, mince & pumpkin pies, puddings
Curry Powder	deviled eggs, sauce for eggs, cottage cheese, cheese sauce	veal croquettes, stews, curried lamb	chicken dishes, fish croquettes, shrimp	
Paprika	scrambled eggs, cottage cheese, Welsh rarebit	Hungarian goulash, gravies, ham	seafood dishes, shell fish, fried chicken	
Poppy Seed	scrambled eggs, omelets, cottage cheese	noodle dishes		coffee cakes, pie, bread, rolls, cookies
Rosemary	deviled eggs, omelets, soufflés	boiled lamb, beef, veal, Swiss steak, pork, pie	capon, pheasant, salmon, baked halibut, chicken	
Dill	deviled eggs, omelets, cottage cheese, macaroni	beef, pot roast, corned beef, lamb chops, pork	chicken pie, baked halibut, lobster, shrimp	
Ginger	cheese dishes	broiled beef, lamb, veal, pot roast, stews, chopped beef	roast chicken, squab, cornish hen	gingerbread, cakes, cookies, pumpkin pie, custards, fruit preserves
Marjoram	soufflés, omelets, creamed eggs, rarebits, cheese sauce	roast beef, pork, veal, stews, loaf, spare ribs	duck, goose, loaf, pheasant, salmon, chicken croquettes	
Mustard	deviled eggs, casseroles, cheese sauces	baked ham, kidneys, pickled meat, sauces	shrimp, creamed & stewed oysters, fish boiled, sauces	molasses cookies, gingerbread
Oregano	creamed eggs, rarebits, cheese sauces scrambled eggs	Swiss steaak, beef stew, broiled & roast lamb, gravies, veal scallopini	Chicken: cacciatore, roast, saute; fish, shrimp and clams	

What If . . . ?

Throughout this book we've discussed various aspects relating to self-sufficiency. One can see the value of a good food storage program and the feeling of satisfaction using it brings.

Yet, in the back of the mind lingers a disquieting thought, "What if. . . ?"

What if you had to evacuate at a moment's notice. What should you take, how long would it take to locate it all, and in what should you carry it?

It doesn't take a fear of war to have these concerns. We read, almost daily, in the newspapers of events that disrupt people's lives:

A number of years ago, in Idaho, an earthen dam broke, triggering a massive flood. People had less than 15 minutes to gather belongings and flee their homes.

Recently an earthquake struck San Francisco, and several others have shaken other cities, tumbling people into the streets in panic.

Most recently, a fire broke out in our neighborhood and authorities were concerned over a possible release of toxic fumes. Three hundred families were forced from their homes that night.

What to do? What to take? The time to plan is now, in the calm atmosphere of forethought.

Consider the most important element: You are thinking SURVIVAL. Survival does not necessarily equate with comfort, else you wouldn't be leaving your home in the first place.

The Three Critical Days

Experience has taught us that it generally takes three days, 72 hours, before government or relief agencies are able to get everything in gear to offer assistance. So, there are three days to plan for. The six important things to provide during this time are:

1) Water
2) A first-aid kit & medicines routinely required
3) Dry clothes
4) Shelter
5) Food
6) A compass, a portable radio and flashlight
(Both with alkaline batteries checked periodically.)

Water should be considered the most essential ingredient of the 72 hour emergency kit, and a minimum of **1 gallon per adult per day** should be included.

First Aid kits should bear in mind injuries that can occur while camping: burns, sprains, blisters, sunburn, and diarrhea. Also, an emergency situation could easily cause stress-related ailments. If you routinely take any medications, such as heart medicines, insulin, or asthma medications, etc., be sure to include these, too.

The following is a list of materials to be included in a first aid kit. This is a bare minimum kit, there are many on the market which contain much more, but consequently require much more space.

Water purification tablets	**First-aid book**	**Gauze roll**
Wood matches, (dipped in paraffin)	**Antiseptic**	**Kaopectate**
	Scissors	**Ace bandage**
Gauze compresses	**Tweezers**	**Sunscreen**
Disinfectant soap	**Vaseline**	**Burn spray**
First Aid cream	**Adhesive tape**	**Aspirin** or **Tylenol**
Thread (for suturing)	**Needles**	

A change of clothes is essential when a person stands a chance of exposure to the elements. Good health is much easier to maintain when the body is kept warm and dry. Be sure to gear your choices to the climatic conditions where you live.

Shelter is required no matter what the climate. In desert areas it affords relief from the sun, and in other climates, from the wind, rain, or snow. It should be kept light. Tube tents and lightweight collapsible nylon tents are available. Even a sheet of 10′ x 6′ plastic can fashion a passable shelter, with the aid of a nylon cord. Heavy sleeping bags can be replaced with lightweight thermal (space) blankets.

Food is placed at the bottom of this list for a reason. Unless there is a pre-existing medical condition or a case of an infant requiring formula, a body could survive three days without eating. As a matter of fact, there are cases of desert survival where the lack of food actually contributed to staying alive. If water is in critical supply, it is further depleted by the act of eating since the body requires water to metabolize the food taken in.

We are in no way advocating doing without food in a 72 hour emergency. This merely explains why it is found at the bottom of the list. Many commercial kits on the market and many published lists of emergency requirements include heavy canned foods, or else dehydrated foods requiring precious water to prepare. The most practical choice, then, would be to purchase the foil packed prepared meals (known as M.R.E.'s for Meals Ready to Eat), intended for military use. They are frequently available at surplus stores, or a similar product may be obtained from stores carrying camping supplies. These are already prepared, requiring no water or refrigeration.

Keep It Portable

Keeping in mind that this is a survival kit, and that survival could very well depend upon how portable the whole collection is kept; being lightweight is crucial. One never knows in an emergency situation if a car would be available.

A good solution is to keep the kits packed in backpacks, scaling the size to the individual. A small child might better carry some of his basic needs in a lap or a fanny pack. Some find it convenient to have their backpacks strapped to a set of luggage wheels, those little foldable carts seen everywhere at airports. This could provide the shoulders a rest during an evacuation. They could also assist in transporting heavy water if it were contained in foldable, plastic 5 gallon containers.

This kit could be personalized for your particular situation, such as baby diapers or sanitary napkins, if needed. (They are also valuable as wound compresses.) It is a "Life Kit", a bare minimum, and will sustain life, though not necessarily, comfort. Make-up, toys, razors, and other extraneous gear would be nice in the comfort of one's home, but an emergency situation requires a bare bones approach or it isn't usable.

Your kit, kept in a known, easily accessible location in the house, could be grabbed in a hurry.

A Kit For The Car

Since emergencies do not always take place when we are at home, a somewhat larger kit could be assembled to be kept in the car. This should include, in addition to the above discussed kit: flares and waterproof matches, keep at least 50 miles worth of gasoline in the tank, tool kit, map of the surrounding area, shovel, jack, and a roll of electrical tape. Desirable, but not essential, would be an extra fan belt, jumper cables, tire chains, tire pump, extra blankets and a hatchet. If room still exists, some extra water is a good idea.

Now that everything is assembled and ready, there is one final thing to which you should give some thought. It doesn't take up much room, and could prove invaluable should family members become separated. Make up copies of birth certificates, insurance policies, wills, and any other important documents, and put them in plastic zip lock bags. Tuck a packet inside each pack and then rest easy. **You are prepared!**

Index

Guide to Recipes of Foods shown in Photographs:

- **Cover Picture -** 100% Whole Wheat Bread, Pg. 39; Colby Cheese, Pg. 123; Rye Berry Pie, Pg. 78
- **A -** Boiled Beans, Pg. 81 & Tofu Sour Cream, Pg. 68; Quesadilla, Pg. 93; "Free For Nothing 'Coffee', Pg. 39; Oat n' Wheat Waffles, Pg. 42; Salisbury Steak & Gravy, Pg. 57; Milk, Milk♥Lite®, Pg. 8, or Soy milk, Pg. 64
- **B -** Southern Cornbread, Pg. 61; Chili-Mac, Pg. 23; Basque Sheepherder Bread, Pg. 35; Chimichangas, Pg. 26 with Tofu Sour Cream, Pg. 68
- **C -** Vegetable Soup, Pg. 140 with Wheat Meatballs, Pg. 56; Tofu-stuffed Green Peppers, Pg. 69; Chimichangas, Pg. 26 with Tofu Sour Cream, Pg. 68; Chocolate Wonder Cake, Pg. 95; Fruit topped Tofu Cheesecake, Pg. 70; Wheat Meat Turkey with Gravy, Pg. 59 and Basic Bread Stuffing, Pg. 149; Fish, See Fish Farming Pg. 114; 100% Whole Wheat Bread, Pg. 39; Prepared Mustard, Pg. 87; Tomato Catsup, Pg. 87; Wheat Meat Hamburger, Pg. 57 with Bun, Pg. 35; Colby Cheese, Pg. 123; Lasagna, Pg. 24
- **D -** Assorted Milk♥Lite® Drinks, Pg. 8
- **E -** Spaghetti & Meatballs, Pgs. 47, 57, 87
- **F -** Oriental-style Wheat Meatball Salad, Pg. 59; "Free for Nothing 'Coffee'", Pg. 39
- **G -** Wheat breads (100% Whole Wheat), Pg. 39; Orange-Flecked Raisin Bread, Pg. 37; French Baguettes, Pg. 36
- **H -** Assorted soaps, Pg. 145

For more information on any item in this book, please write:

P. O. Box 2050
Higley, AZ 85236-2050